# How to Start a Private Practice

Starting a private medical practice offers physicians and other allied health professionals unparalleled autonomy over clinical decisions, practice management, and work–life balance. This independence allows practitioners to develop personalized treatment approaches and stronger patient relationships without corporate constraints, often resulting in higher satisfaction for both medical professionals and patients. Financially, private practices can be more lucrative through direct control of revenue streams and business operations. Beyond personal benefits, private practices are vital to healthcare ecosystems by providing community-centered care, increasing access in underserved areas, and fostering innovation through a nimble adaptation to emerging healthcare needs. In an era of increasing healthcare consolidation, independent practices preserve the essential doctor–patient relationship that forms the foundation of quality healthcare delivery.

*How to Start a Private Practice* is a comprehensive guide for physicians, dentists, mental health professionals, physical therapists, and other allied health practitioners seeking to transition from residency, fellowship, or corporate practice into a private practice setting. Written by experienced physicians Bertrand Liang, MD, PhD, and Mitchell Liester, MD, this practical guidebook provides a road map for establishing, managing, and growing a successful private practice in today's complex healthcare landscape.

This book provides physicians and other allied health practitioners with a step-by-step guide to establishing and managing a successful private practice. The authors combine business fundamentals with healthcare-specific knowledge to help medical practitioners navigate the complexities of practice ownership. This comprehensive approach, from addressing psychological barriers to providing detailed guidance on coding and billing, ensures that readers will have the tools they need to succeed in today's challenging healthcare environment.

# How to Start a Private Practice

## A Guide for Clinicians and Providers

Bertrand Liang, MD, PhD and Mitchell Liester, MD

Routledge
Taylor & Francis Group
A PRODUCTIVITY PRESS BOOK

Designed cover image: Shutterstock

First published 2026
by Routledge
605 Third Avenue, New York, NY 10158

and by Routledge
4 Park Square, Milton Park, Abingdon, Oxon, OX14 4RN

*Routledge is an imprint of the Taylor & Francis Group, an informa business*



ISBN: 978-1-041-16647-4 (hbk)
ISBN: 978-1-041-16646-7 (pbk)
ISBN: 978-1-003-68562-3 (ebk)

DOI: 10.4324/9781003685623

Typeset in Garamond
by Newgen Publishing UK

We dedicate this book to all clinicians who serve their patients, no matter what environment they choose to pursue their practice.

# Contents

# Authors

**Bertrand Liang**, MD, PhD, is a board-certified neurologist and fellow, American Academy of Neurology, who has successfully operated a private practice after transitioning from academic medicine. He is currently a faculty member in the Department of Neurology at the teaching program of St. Joseph Medical Center, where he acts as a mentor for residents, as well as in the Department of Neurology at the Anschutz School of Medicine of the University of Colorado, with emphasis on medical student teaching. Dr. Liang brings a wealth of experience in the business aspects of medicine. He has published over 80 peer-reviewed articles in leading medical journals, 12 chapters in medical textbooks, and 4 books, including 2 business-related books: *Managing and Leading for Science Professionals* (2014) and *Pragmatic MBA for the Scientific and Technical Executive* (2013). He was elected a fellow of the American Academy of Neurology due to his exemplary achievements in neurology, as well as a nominating member, Sigma Xi, the research honor society, due to his long history of basic and clinical research. Dr. Liang maintains an active teaching schedule, focusing on clinical medicine and physician entrepreneurship. He writes actively on "Medium", which reaches over 25,000 monthly readers. Dr. Liang is an alumnus of the Feinberg School of Medicine at Northwestern University, the Institute of Materials Research and Innovation, University of Bolton, the Law School at the University of London/Queen Mary, the MIT Sloan School of Management, as well as programs in internal medicine at Brown University; Neurology, Oncology and Molecular Genetics at the University of Michigan; with studies in molecular biology and genetics at the National Center for Human Genome Sciences and the National Cancer Institute.

**Mitchell B. Liester**, MD, is a board-certified psychiatrist and Assistant Clinical Professor at the University of Colorado School of Medicine, where he has been recognized with the Outstanding Clinical Teacher Award. With over 35 years of clinical experience, Dr. Liester combines traditional psychiatric practice with groundbreaking research in consciousness studies, psychedelic medicine, and innovative therapeutic approaches. As a prolific researcher and author, Dr. Liester has published over 30 peer-reviewed articles in leading medical and psychiatric journals, focusing on novel treatments for treatment-resistant depression, consciousness studies, and the therapeutic applications of psychedelic medicine. His pioneering work includes research on low-dose sublingual ketamine therapy, personality changes following organ transplantation, and the therapeutic potential of psychoplastogens. He has also contributed a chapter to *The Therapeutic Use of Ayahuasca* (2013) and has presented his research at numerous national and international conferences, including the World Congress of Psychiatry and European Congress of Psychiatry. Dr. Liester serves as a thought leader in the field through his popular *Psychology Today* blog, "The Leading Edge", which has garnered over 300,000 reads since its launch in 2024. His 50 published blog posts explore cutting-edge topics in mental health, consciousness, and innovative treatments. He is also a sought-after podcast guest and has created educational video content on ketamine therapy. In addition to his clinical practice, Dr. Liester has held leadership positions, including vice president of the International Association for Near-Death Studies and serves as a peer reviewer for multiple medical journals. He is actively involved in medical education, serving as a psychiatric preceptor for medical students at the Anschutz School of Medicine of the University of Colorado.

# Preface

When we entered medical school, we had a simple dream: to become skilled physicians who could help patients navigate their health challenges. Like most of our classmates, we focused intensely on mastering anatomy, pharmacology, and the countless other disciplines required to practice medicine. After years of training, we emerged ready to heal – but completely unprepared for the business side of medicine.

This reality faces virtually every physician. We spend over a decade in rigorous medical training yet receive almost no education on how to run a practice. For generations, new doctors simply joined established groups where they could learn the business aspects through apprenticeship. Today, as more physicians find themselves in corporate medical environments that prioritize productivity over autonomy, "churn" over compassion, many yearn for independence but don't know where to begin.

This book was born from countless conversations with colleagues who expressed the same sentiment: "I'd start my own practice if I only knew how". Time and again, we've heard brilliant clinicians – specialists at the top of their field – admit they feel intimidated by the prospect of running a business. The vocabulary seems foreign, the processes mysterious, and the risks terrifying.

Yet the irony is striking. If you've mastered the intricacies of complex medical conditions, you absolutely have the intellectual capacity to understand business fundamentals. The concepts in this book are far less complex than the medical knowledge you've already conquered. The difference is simply exposure and familiarity.

We have traveled different paths to successful private practices. We've made mistakes, learned valuable lessons, and ultimately created sustainable practices that allow us to practice medicine on our own terms. In writing this guide, we've distilled decades of experience into practical, actionable steps that demystify every aspect of starting and running a medical practice.

Our goal is not to convince every physician to open a private practice. For some, employment within a larger system is the right choice. But we aim to remove the knowledge barrier that prevents many physicians from considering private practice as a viable option. In today's healthcare landscape, with physician burnout at unprecedented levels, having choices matters more than ever.

The chapters ahead will walk you through everything from confronting initial fears to mastering medical billing. We've included practical checklists, timelines, and templates you can immediately implement. Most important, we've written this guide in plain language, translating business concepts into terms familiar to physicians.

Whether you're a resident contemplating your first position, a mid-career physician feeling trapped in corporate medicine, or any student or provider simply curious about your options, this book provides the road map you've been seeking. The journey to practice independence isn't always easy, but it's far more accessible than you might think.

As you turn these pages, remember that starting a private practice isn't just about business – it's about reclaiming the joy of medicine and practicing in alignment with your personal values. In a healthcare system that increasingly treats physicians as interchangeable assets, private practice offers the opportunity to create the kind of medicine you envisioned when you first donned your white coat.

The path to practice ownership begins here. Let's take the first step together.

# Acknowledgments

It takes a village to create anything new, and this book is no exception. Many clinicians provided anecdotes of their experiences and the challenges they did (or anticipate they will) face, both in private practice and those in corporate practice; we thank them for speaking to us. For commentary and reviewing chapters and in some cases the entire text, we thank Casey Dolan, MD; Andrew Hull, MS4; Kate Liang, MPH; Jon Konzen, DO; and John Kao, MD. For their thoughts, concerns, and conceptualization of the future in which they will be practicing, we thank the many residents with whom we spoke at St. Joseph Medical Center and UC Davis programs. From those about to enter into the next phases of their medical careers, the University of Colorado medical students at Mission Medical Center provided (and continue to provide) undying enthusiasm and perspective. For many discussions about practice structure, we thank Jean Sun, MD, and Jose Carrau-Lebron, MD, and for his wise advice and support during the creative process, we thank Sid Gilman, MD. Finally and most important, we thank our spouses, Diane and Paula, who tolerated time away physically and mentally while engaging in this project, and without whom this book would never have become a reality. Thanks to you all.

# Acknowledgments

# Chapter 1

# Confronting Fears

For years, you've trained tirelessly. You've endured long nights, grueling shifts, and the relentless pressure of medical residency or corporate practice. You have sacrificed time, energy, and personal pursuits to achieve your dream of becoming a physician. The journey has been one of discipline, endurance, and immense learning. Now, as you stand at the crossroads of your career, an undeniable thought keeps surfacing: *What if I went out on my own?*

The idea of starting a solo private practice is exhilarating – offering autonomy, financial potential, and the ability to practice medicine on your terms. The notion of being your own boss, crafting the patient experience, and making decisions without corporate oversight is deeply appealing. Yet, alongside that excitement is a deeper, often paralyzing fear. What if it doesn't work? What if I'm making a mistake? What if I fail?

You are not alone in feeling this way. In fact, the uncertainty and anxiety you face are normal. Many highly trained and competent physicians experience hesitation when considering such a significant shift. This chapter will explore these fears, both conscious and unconscious, and provide strategies to overcome them so you can move forward with confidence. You have already achieved so much; now it is time to take control of your career and future. Besides, you didn't survive medical school, residency, and those dreaded 3 AM calls just to let fear stop you now!

## The Conscious Fears: The Ones You Acknowledge

Some fears are obvious, tangible, and easy to name. They often stem from legitimate concerns about business, finances, and personal security.

Financial uncertainty is one of the most common fears. The unpredictable income in the beginning stages of private practice can feel daunting. Concerns about overhead costs, staff salaries, and revenue generation are common. Physicians transitioning from salaried positions to private practice

DOI: 10.4324/9781003685623-1

often feel as though they're walking a tightrope without a safety net. The key to overcoming this fear is strategic financial planning. Having savings in place, securing initial funding, and creating a realistic budget can provide reassurance during the early stages. Importantly, having guidance to give comfort to your decision is key. Like learning any new skill or vocabulary, once it's done, it doesn't seem so overwhelming.

Lack of business knowledge is another significant concern. Many physicians are unfamiliar with the logistics of running a business – billing, marketing, compliance, and operational management. Unlike patient care, which has been ingrained through years of training, the business side of medicine is often foreign territory. Fortunately, business acumen can be learned, and there are resources available, including practice consultants, financial advisors, and professional networks that can help bridge this knowledge gap. Again, once using the parlance and processes it becomes more familiar and less daunting – just another "system" that can become familiar.

Fear of losing patients or referrals is another challenge. Transitioning from an employed position to an independent practice, for example, raises concerns about patient retention and maintaining referral relationships. Many physicians worry that without the backing of a large institution, their patient flow will diminish. However, providing excellent care, maintaining strong communication with referring providers, and marketing strategically can ensure a steady patient base. Personal relationships with patients and colleagues are invaluable in establishing credibility. In fact, the other aspect is the lack of physicians/providers that not only is present now but is also anticipated to continue for many years. The services we provide – no matter what type of medicine we practice – are and will be in need. A shortage of patients is *not* a likely scenario in the present and upcoming future.

Regulatory and legal concerns can also be overwhelming. Healthcare compliance, malpractice insurance, and credentialing requirements can feel like a bureaucratic nightmare. However, breaking the process down into manageable steps and seeking expert guidance can make it significantly less intimidating. Having a legal or compliance specialist consultant can ensure all requirements are met and reduce unnecessary stress. The stepwise process isn't difficult – in fact, it is similar to what even corporate medicine positions require for providers to undergo. So if you've already been already been in practice, you know those steps. Otherwise while there are advisors who can help you with this, they may even fall into the rubric of a centralized process (e.g., Council for Affordable Quality Healthcare [CAQH]). Many practices find *Healthcare Compliance Pros* valuable for its combined focus on compliance and comparative data.

## The Unconscious Fears: The Ones That Hold You Back

Beyond the obvious worries, there are deeper, often unspoken fears that can prevent a physician from making the leap into solo practice.

Fear of failure and judgment is common. Many physicians worry about the stigma of failing in business and the judgment from colleagues. The thought of venturing out, taking a risk, and possibly falling short can be intimidating. Nonetheless, there are ways we mitigate risk, reducing our chances of failure. The whole purpose of this book is to provide you an overview of how to set up things so you don't fail. The key is to prepare and note that hiccups are possible but not fatal to your efforts.

Imposter syndrome is another powerful, internalized fear. Self-doubt can creep in, making even the most competent physicians question their ability to run a successful practice. The little voice inside whispers, "Who am *I* to do this?" Recognizing that these thoughts are normal – and actively countering them with positive reinforcement – is crucial. Surrounding yourself with mentors and peers who encourage and validate your capabilities can help silence this doubt.

Fear of losing work–life balance can be a legitimate concern. Managing all aspects of a practice can feel like an insurmountable burden, leading to worries about personal time and burnout. However, private practice also offers the opportunity to design a schedule that works for you. By hiring capable support staff, setting boundaries, and using technology to streamline administrative tasks, physicians can maintain a healthy work–life balance.

## Overcoming the Fear: Strategies for Moving Forward

Recognizing these fears is the first step in overcoming them. The next step is to develop a plan to address them head-on.

Educating yourself and building a support system is crucial. There are a number of strategies, which we'll cover in this book. There are many resources available for medical professionals venturing into private practice, from industry-specific consultants to business-focused medical associations. By reading this book, you will learn the steps you can take to build a successful practice.

Starting small and planning strategically can help mitigate risks. We'll cover various aspects, like considering starting part-time or sharing an office space before expanding, or being solo and/or having a small staff initially. Step-by-step growth will allow you to grow your practice at a manageable rate.

Addressing financial fears with a solid business plan is essential. Outline a clear roadmap with expense estimates, projected revenue, and funding sources. Financial literacy in general is important for you for your practice, as well as for your personal life. We'll cover this in subsequent chapters as well as strategies for creating a business plan and guidance for how you can use it to build your successful private practice.

Shifting your mindset to view setbacks as part of growth is another powerful tool. Many successful physicians had initial challenges before thriving in private practice. The key is persistence and adaptability. Every issue presents a learning opportunity that ultimately contributes to long-term success.

Recognizing your strengths and skills can make all the difference. Focus on what you do best – patient care. Business expertise can be learned, as can the administrative, and help can be rented or hired. You don't have to do everything alone; delegation and collaboration are key to sustainable success.

Setting boundaries to maintain work–life balance ensures longevity in private practice. Implementing efficient workflows, delegating tasks, and setting clear work hours can help avoid burnout. Being proactive about managing time will allow you to enjoy both professional satisfaction and personal fulfillment.

## Conclusion: Fear Is Normal, But It Shouldn't Stop You

Fear is a natural response to stepping outside your comfort zone, but it should not be the reason you stay in a situation that doesn't fulfill you. Many physicians who have made the transition to private practice look back and wonder why they didn't do it sooner. The rewards of autonomy, professional satisfaction, and a healthier work–life balance far outweigh the risks.

*So take the leap. You survived residency – you can thrive in this. You are capable, and your future patients are waiting!*

# Chapter 2

# Lessons Learned

You don't have to figure out how to start a solo private practice all by yourself. (After all, that's the purpose of this book!). Countless other physicians before you have opened and built successful private practices. You can learn from them and us – both the successes and the mistakes, and how well we can anticipate either.

*Dr. Liester:* For example, one of us was from a family of educators, not doctors. My family had no physicians in it, just teachers. So when it came to medicine and starting a private solo practice, I was clueless. And then, just to make life more challenging, I decided to become a psychiatrist. We didn't have any of those in my family either! In fact, I had never met or worked with a psychiatrist and hadn't even seen one before entering medical school. So, I was totally in the dark about how to build a psychiatric practice.

After completing my psychiatric residency, I decided that rather than accepting a position in academia when it was offered, I would leave and try something totally different. Academia had become comfortable after four years of medical school and four years of psychiatric residency. But I chose to leave that familiar setting and instead venture out into something new and different. I accepted an employed position at a community mental health clinic, an environment I had never worked in previously and really knew nothing about. What was I thinking?!

Knowing nothing about a new position can be both a blessing and a curse – a blessing because you don't necessarily know what you are up against, and a curse because you don't know what you are up against!

The community mental health clinic where I chose to work was in my hometown. I had moved away 12 years earlier to pursue my education – this included 4 years each of undergraduate studies, medical school, and residency. Eight of those years were spent in other states (I am from Colorado but completed my undergraduate degree in Arizona and residency in California). I wanted to familiarize myself with the resources in my community as well as the laws pertaining to mental health, which vary from state to state. A guaranteed salary and benefits, which included health insurance,

 DOI: 10.4324/9781003685623-2

paid time off, and a predictable schedule, all sounded appealing coming out of a four-year residency that included regular overnight call, long work hours, and the internal politics inherent in every academic institution. So, I accepted the contract the community health clinic offered. I never even considered negotiating the specifics of that contract or having it reviewed by an attorney. I was fresh out of residency and had to start paying back my medical school student loans that were deferred during residency. Also, my wife and I were buying a new house and it seemed like a waste of money to pay someone to read a contract that appeared so simple and straight forward.

But soon after starting in my new position, things began to change. I should have paid more attention to what the clinic director who hired me said. She told me that psychiatrists didn't tend to stay long in my position. They all left for the greener pastures of private practice. I assumed this was because they saw an opportunity to make more money, and since that wasn't my focus, I was certain that I would stick around. I liked being part of a team, and I was happy with the salary they offered me. They were going to pay me much more than I had earned in jobs during high school or college, which paid close to minimum wage, and it was three times higher than what I earned as a resident! It seemed like an enormous amount of money, and I was glad they thought I was worth that much!

I had been hired for a specific role in the mental health system, but it soon became apparent that there were significant shortages of psychiatrists in other areas of this system. Before long, I was asked to "help" the clinic by assuming additional responsibilities. Someone was needed to oversee patients in the residential treatment program, so I agreed to take on that role. Then, there was a shortage of psychiatrists in the outpatient clinic. I was a "team player", so I agreed to help with that position also. Oh yes, and they needed someone to go to two hospitals to take care of the patients who required inpatient treatment. That seemed a bit daunting, but I was young and energetic, and besides, they offered to have a nurse help me with the patients. So, I took on that job as well. Before long, I was doing the work of four psychiatrists, without any change in compensation. Instead, what I received was frustration and criticism from the clinic director who hired me because I was not in her department enough to provide the help she expected from me.

It didn't take long for me to burn out. Less than a year after being hired, I resigned from this position. Then I learned the same problems that caused me to leave had caused the psychiatrist who preceded me to quit, and later, the two psychiatrists who stepped into that same role after me left for the same reasons!

At that point in my life, I was 31 years old and was newly married to a physician who was pregnant with our first child. The thought of leaving a salaried position for an uncertain future was terrifying, but I knew that I wouldn't survive if I stayed in the employed position I had just left. So I took the leap and started a solo private practice – and I have never regretted it!

My first step was to find an office for this fledgling new private practice. Fortunately, a colleague was also looking for an office and was willing to share space, which lowered the overhead for both of us. We found a location we both liked, and I took out a bank loan to pay for my half of the office furniture, as well as the office supplies that I needed to get started. I was amazed that a bank was willing to loan me money; after all, I was less than one year out of residency. What I didn't know then was that banks love to loan money to doctors! They see us as very good customers. Next, I found a family friend who was willing to help me by working part time to help with medical transcription, billing, and various additional office duties. She was a wonderful human being and a good friend, so I overlooked the fact that she had no previous experience in medical billing.

The next step was to find patients for my new private practice. I knew nothing about marketing, but the two hospitals where I worked previously while employed by the mental health clinic were always looking for new psychiatrists to admit and treat people on their inpatient units. This brought in more business to their facilities and reduced the number of on-call nights for the other psychiatrists who were on staff there.

So, I began taking overnight calls, which were as so much easier than being on call as a resident. About one night each week, I took phone calls at home from the admissions staff. They were tasked with evaluating patients who had come to their emergency room or admissions unit seeking inpatient treatment. The staff did most of the work. They evaluated the patients and determined if they needed inpatient treatment. If they decided inpatient treatment was appropriate, they would call me and present the case, then ask if I would accept the patient. If I did, then I simply called admission orders to the inpatient unit and saw the patient the next day. This call was a breeze compared to residency, when I had to sleep at the hospital and was repeatedly woken up to go to the emergency room and conduct a psychiatric evaluation to determine whether the patients required hospitalization.

Private practice call was so much easier! I could take the call from home and didn't have to go to the hospital until the next day. Also, many of these patients were admitted voluntarily – they were asking for help – as opposed to the patients I encountered during residency who often were brought in by the police or family members. They were not happy about being there and often were uncooperative with the evaluation and the recommendation for hospitalization. This necessitated placing them on a 72-hour involuntary hold, which legally forced them to be admitted and receive treatment. This adversarial relationship was stressful, and I did not enjoy it. To work with cooperative patients who were actually asking for help was a dream come true!

In addition, the vast majority of patients who were admitted to the hospital, either voluntarily or involuntarily, did not have an outpatient psychiatrist. So, once they were stabilized and were discharged from the hospital, I had a steady stream of patients coming to see me for outpatient follow-up treatment. With this arrangement, my practice filled up rapidly with cooperative patients who wanted to get better.

It wasn't long before physicians in the community learned of the "new psychiatrist in town" and began referring patients. Also, satisfied patients began telling their friends and soon more patients called looking for psychiatric treatment. (It turns out, word-of-mouth referrals from satisfied patients are one of the most effective marketing tools). So, it wasn't long before I had to begin limiting how many new patients I accepted into the practice to avoid being overwhelmed. It is scary as a new doctor to turn away referrals. I wondered, would other physicians stop referring to me if I didn't accept their referrals? Would the word-of-mouth referrals dry up? Would my practice languish as my current patients improved and no longer needed treatment? The answer is a resounding "no!" It turns out that having a thriving practice only increases demand for your services.

I was fortunate to work with wonderful patients and the vast majority of them improved over time. When some had progressed to the point they no longer required psychiatric care, I began drawing from a waiting list of patients who had called seeking an appointment when my practice was full. This allowed me to remain as busy as I wanted to be. This is the key to what we term the flexibility of private practice – we structure how we want to work and how much and can emphasize our work–life balance.

*Dr. Liang:* I had a different pathway. Instead of going into an employed position in a clinic, academic medicine was where I started. I had already been practicing in the world of the federal government at governmental facilities, so I knew the type of patients, their needs, and the rough infrastructure that was required, from furniture to an infusion center for the administration of IV drugs. I also knew of the competition and the insecurities of some of the other less specialized doctors within the federal system. When I left that practice to go into academia, I thought I was well-armed with the need to have to set up something new.

However, when I first arrived at my first academic job, I realized that no contracts had been set up and that only my general clinic had been scheduled, not my specialty clinic. I sought out the advice of previous mentors to understand the process of getting reimbursement contracts and spent the next month negotiating with the various third-party payers, noting the level of reimbursement, time to payment, as well as the number of patients in each of the insurance plans that were available, and arranged for "slots" to be filled of each depending on their reimbursement. I also was sure to obtain their policies for my "procedure" (IV drug infusion) to be clear how and when reimbursement was going to occur. This allowed me to predict the levels of income I could anticipate being brought into the practice.

This was great training for the future. I was able to build a practice by initially creating the appropriate infrastructure, and then obtaining my reimbursement contracts, and only then seeing patients. I was making a lot of money for the hospital and the department but was still the lowest ranking faculty despite generating the most revenue – and the irony was that all the "scut" work of extra coverage, or committee meetings no one wanted to go to, or other non-reimbursed activities were falling to me. I realized that I had done the work but had not enjoyed the spoils of a private practice.

I also began having the symptoms of burnout. Since I was the only one with my subspecialty, I was expected to be available 24/7 for questions in the area, for patients who were admitted to the hospital, and for consults in the hospital and other clinics. In addition, the teaching and research responsibilities continued to pile up, with the pressures of generating income from seeing patients, ancillary activities (e.g., prescribing infusional drugs), and grant writing consuming literally all of my waking (and often sleeping!) hours. At that point I wondered if medicine really was the right field for me.

That's when others started recruiting me. I saw that options were available, and that my value was higher than what my initial job had been giving me credit. That job then began offering things to me to try to entice me to stay, but with little contractual support nor commitment. As a result I jumped at the opportunity to go elsewhere where the reimbursement, and the negotiated percentage of revenues for me which was "impossible" at my last job, became a formal written reality, along with much more control of my time. I was actually the leader of the group, which was also an eye-opening experience. The fact was that there had been no leadership before, and there was a significant amount of chaos as a result. It taught me a very good lesson – there always needs to be a single chief, since if there isn't there is a degeneration of relationships from everyone thinking they are the most important, rather than the overall health of the group.

In fact, one practice that I was recruited to had exactly this problem. They hired a "COO" to try to herd the cats of the group of ten providers. But all of them had their own electronic health records (EHRs), their own accounts payable groups, their own ancillary staff – so it was not so much a practice as it was a bunch of individual practices, which squabbled about who was using the most internet, or parking, or expense of rent (two of the partners owned the building, and the remaining eight had to pay rent to those two). The COO finally became so tired of not being able to create an economy of scale or modify resource utilization that he just quit. I watched this from an arm's length while being recruited and witnessed the potential of decreasing overhead and increasing profitability only to be lost due to inability to have defined leadership. And that practice no longer exists. Although I did temporarily rejoin a practice that was similar but under the rubric of a corporate practice, I saw once again the ridiculous requirements of corporate medicine, the continued addition of uncompensated work required, and the "policies" that were made to make money for the hospitals at the expense of the providers. And I saw providers who were unhappy, afraid, burnt out, and realized I knew I had to go back to private practice.

Today my private practice is thriving. I work when I want, have full control of my schedule, have a great work–life balance, and have fantastic professional relationships that are fulfilling and continue to challenge me. The patients for whom I care, and the trainees such as residents and students, all have added to the private practice experience allowing me to be the best doctor I can be, and continue to have fun giving back and learning. And I realize I am fortunate enough to have realized the benefits before I burnt out, and unlike others I've seen, have quit with bitterness and disparagement.

*Dr. Liester:* After several decades of providing psychiatric care to adolescents and adults, I began to feel that my clinical practice had become somewhat stagnant or routine. I no longer felt challenged by the cases I was seeing. Although I continued to enjoy my patients and supporting their progress, I began to feel as if I could provide these services in my sleep. My practice was becoming rote, routine, and somewhat boring. That is when I decided to make changes.

I took a position as a volunteer faculty member with a local medical school. This allowed me to interact with other faculty and teach medical students, which I continue to find stimulating and enjoyable. I also began involving medical students in research projects, which helped them in their careers and was fun for me as well. I began volunteering one half day a month at a local medical clinic for patients who do not have insurance. These patients are grateful for the care they receive, which is rewarding, and it also allowed me to meet other dedicated physicians who volunteer in the clinic. I continue to learn an enormous amount from these physicians, and in addition, we get to teach medical students in the clinic, as well as interact with pharmacy students. It is a dynamic teaching environment where we all learn from each other.

I also began to explore new treatment options by communicating with physicians locally, nationally, and internationally who are using novel therapies to successfully treat psychiatric and other medical disorders. I began publishing case reports and scientific papers and presenting at medical conferences around the world. This exposed me to new treatment modalities that I had not known about previously. Then I started writing a blog, which is something I never thought I would do, and I love it! This allows me to explore topics in psychiatry and medicine that I think about often, but did not have an outlet for sharing with others. Now, I hear from readers who share my interest in these topics, which has resulted in the blossoming of new friendships and new opportunities for additional collaboration. These new activities are exciting, educational, and enjoyable. They have rejuvenated me to the point that I am now having the most fun I have ever had in my 40 years of clinical practice!

*Dr. Liang:* I had also engaged with teaching and research allowing a whole new avenue of private practice. We both volunteer to teach medical students on a local level, and I also have the privilege of being a mentor to many residents who I have been able to teach in a new program in the West. I've been able to combine my experiences and collaborate with other clinicians toward new ideas for the future, both in the realm of clinical research but also in the area of resident and student education, allowing me to give back to our collective community.

The irony is that when I tried to do some of these types of things in the corporate practice of medicine, it was actively frowned upon and discouraged, thought to be a waste of time, with very specific negative views on teaching and having students and residents rotate with us. The mission was to make money for the hospital/corporate system, rather than be involved in being an example for the next generation of physicians/providers, being something greater than oneself, helping others achieve their goals. Again, that's just not the rubric of corporate medicine – and your choices of your activities are at best limited and constricted. The key is not necessarily to be a mentor to or teacher of others, but to have the ability to formulate *your* practice the way *you* want it to be.

Private practice affords the most beneficial aspects of flexibility in the world of medicine.

## Lessons Learned

Although both of us have been fortunate to build successful private practices, neither can claim this was due to intelligence, skill, or superb planning. Much of the success of our practices has resulted from stumbling forward and learning from choices – both those that worked and those that didn't work. It also helps to work in a high-demand specialty (psychiatry and neurology/neuro-oncology) where there is a shortage of providers (although today, that's pretty much *every* therapeutic area). Also, while a psychiatric practice does not have high overhead expenses, a neurology practice certainly can, of which much needs to be planned. If doing it over again there are certainly many things to be done differently.

For example, never accept a job without clearly understanding and negotiating the employment contract before signing it. A lack of clarity about job responsibilities resulted in dissatisfaction for everyone involved, particularly with respect to expectations. Doing one's homework is also incredibly important on those who have had similar positions and/or worked with the practice previously. The key is to be prepared to negotiate a contract up front, rather than accept what is considered "standard" – that typically means something good for the hospital/practice and not good for the physician/provider. READ. YOUR. CONTRACT. (This will be noted again and again!) If you don't understand it, find counsel who does and can advise you – there are plenty of legal services specifically for physician contracts available today. Don't shortchange yourself.

Next, if asked to accept responsibilities that exceeded those specified in an employment contract, the employment contract should be re-negotiated to reflect those changes. Being fresh out of residency, or even coming from a corporate practice, many physicians are reluctant to stand up for themselves. But as a physician, you hold a great deal of power and *have the obligation* to request changes to your contract if your employer changes their expectations, such as asking you to assume additional responsibilities (a common tactic in corporate medicine). However, the best way to mitigate this is to read your contract up front, have an employment attorney read it, and anticipate needing to change the first offer to ensure it is clear what the roles and responsibilities are of the physician/provider. Too many providers we know personally signed contracts without reading them, to their serious detriment, and only afforded limited options when asked to help with their particular plight.

When transitioning to private practice, a business plan often is not created; this is why it is one of the first chapters in this book. Your practice needs to generate a profit, which is a planned activity. Knowing nothing about finance created a stumbling meander through the financial aspects of running a practice. Having a business plan would have made it much easier to forecast for the future and have a clearer sense of how the practice was doing financially. Again, this is why we believe finance and the business plan – which are not hard to understand or create – are early in this book.

Another lesson learned is to hire experts, rather than friends, unless they are experienced in the area for which they're being hired. Although in the example given my friend was a wonderful person and extremely helpful in other areas, her inexperience as a medical biller resulted in a loss of income for the practice. The practice is a business and has to be treated as such with the best expertise obtained for any aspect that you yourself are not directly responsible.

Also, if starting over, finding more ways to collaborate with other physicians earlier in a career would be a priority. Being in solo private practice can be isolating. Despite the numerous advantages that come with being your own boss, such as having complete control over your schedule, the freedom to take time off whenever you like, a higher income than if working in an employed position, etc., it is easy to become isolated from your peers. However, if you've written out your marketing plan, part of what you will be doing is direct "selling", by giving talks at the hospital, or doing credentialing, or giving talks to laypeople on your area of expertise. Nonetheless, consider other activities if you feel these are important to you; teaching, volunteering, presenting at conferences, etc. at an earlier point in a career can potentially enrich the experience as a physician and create more of a balance in a career. It doesn't necessarily have to be these things, but finding other outlets of your talents can make the physician/provider aspect even more satisfying, especially with the flexibility of being in private practice. Indeed, one of us also gives informational talks to first responders about emergencies in our specific therapeutic area, as well as advocacy work at the Federal level for physician-related issues.

Finally, it is important to remember to balance personal and family time with the demands of any private practice. When you are the doctor and the business owner, it is very easy to spend more and more time working while spending less and less time with family and friends. This can create an unhealthy work–life imbalance that can be disastrous for your relationships as well as your physical and mental health. Planning your time carefully, from patient care to business care, and reserving time for yourself, your family, and other important parts of living, is something you can control better than if you were in a corporate practice where you are told what to do, when to do it, and by when. Remember, you are in a marathon, not a sprint, and although it may sound like a cliché, it is important to enjoy the ride!

# Chapter 3

# Overview and Path

Ok, so you've decided you're interested in starting a private practice – wonderful! The fruits of your labor will translate directly back to you, and with a little bit of planning, you can start this venture with confidence, alacrity, and be a true resource for your community. This overview will help with a thought process and provide a pathway toward making your practice a reality. Note that more details about each component will be found in ensuing chapters.

## Planning

Why planning? Running any type of business, whether it's your own home to a mega-million dollar operation, is basically the same – you want to make sure your revenues are greater than your expenses, and you stay within your means. Don't worry – we're going to go over a lot of this so you can know what you need to approach as well as how. And the flexibility you derive is based on what you plan and what *you* want, not a nameless corporate edict that comes down from who knows where.

## Initial Questions

In general, the first thing you need to do is to determine who your patients are. Ask yourself the following questions:

1. *What's the product that you're offering?* It'll be different if you're procedure oriented vs. outpatient focused. You should know what you've done in your practice to date (whether that's been 20 years at a group, or coming out of residency or fellowship) and what you enjoy doing.
2. *What is the "market segment" you are trying to address?* This has four components:

DOI: 10.4324/9781003685623-3

   a. Adequate size: Make sure you have enough patients to be able to keep you busy. In general, this is typically not a problem with virtually any provider.
   b. Accessibility: You should be able to target this population of patients with any marketing you do. Make sure you tie this into *how* you want to let your target patients know about your practice, and the ability of patients to be able to access your practice.
   c. Measurability: Be able to define the market potential, vis-a-vis other market segments that you DON'T want to currently approach.
   d. Response to "marketing mix". Ensure you have an idea, based on your previous experience, whether this group will respond to what you have to offer once they hear about it. How will your outreach, whether by advertising, social media, in person interaction, be received?
3. *What benefits do you anticipate to be received by the patient?* This is a key component, since your patients will also be part of your word of mouth marketing, and what you can articulate in your own efforts going forward. While improvement of overall health is a given (after all, that's what we do for a living!), also think about satisfaction, health maintenance, mindset, etc.
4. *Describe the "economic utility" of your practice.* In our case, this is also fourfold in nature and encompasses how to deliver your offering to your market segment.
   a. Form utility: Communication of what your market segment wants from the practice (e.g., expertise in a given area, or availability within a certain timeframe).
   b. Place utility: The location where your market segment can purchase your offering (e.g., convenient location for a given demographic).
   c. Time utility: The time in which your product is available for purchase (e.g., full-time outpatient scheduled 8 AM–5 PM six days a week, or one day a week in a given office of several, AM hours only).
   d. Information utility: Communication of information to the market segment members to understand the offering and to make a decision to purchase (e.g., social media targeting of services to a given demographic).

Now, a word about marketing. Marketing in its simplest form is the communication of product attributes that satisfy a customer need. This takes on various forms, from print media, to social media, to word-of-mouth message dissemination, etc. In today's world, referrals from other providers to the presence on the internet are *de rigueur* and fortunately can be managed with a variety of different third-party means. We as providers don't have to be afraid of this since it is something that can be outsourced very effectively with other services (e.g., customer relationship management, or CRM – covered in a later chapter). Moreover, *the need for physician services far outstrips the supply*, and a marketing plan can be developed effectively understanding the demographics of your local area. Many vendors are available to help with this effort.

Nonetheless, by answering the four questions above, you have effectively begun your own marketing research and how to address the patient population you wish to serve. Write it out; that's the basis of your first step in planning. Congratulations!

## Specifics: Drilling Down

Now let's go into some specifics on your practice. This will help you identify the type of practice you want to set up, as well as some infrastructure requirements. In marketing parlance, let's go over "The Four Ps".

## Product

Seems pretty simple – you want to offer medical services one way or another. But let's get more granular about this – the who, what, where, and how. Any service/product you want to offer may be broad, but what do you want to emphasize? This is called positioning – what characteristics are being stressed of your offering? Are you interested in doing primarily geriatrics? Or maybe you want to do primarily GI surgery. Maybe you want to do health prevention alone, or more holistic medicine. In any event, note in particular what are the primary characteristics you want to emphasize, and then the secondary ones, such as perhaps weight loss, or a given set of comorbidities, for example.

Further, are you looking to service only a given community, or are you a superspecialist who people from outside the area need to access? Relatedly, do you want to service outside areas with multiple offices, or offer telemedicine services? When you've dived into these, it helps both with positioning but also with how you will differentiate yourself. Finally, this will allow you to see the competitive landscape that exists – who else is offering what you do? How are you different?

## Place

As noted, where you decide to practice is one component. Your specific practice will dictate whether you want to immediately have multiple offices, or stick with one and provide another type of venue (e.g., telemedicine) to access additional patients. There are a myriad of different options that will be described when it comes to place, from the standard solo practitioner office to shared space medical office space that is "rented" for short periods of time. As a practitioner, you need to decide how you want to make your offering available to your market segment, noting often times patients will associate you with the location and physical plant you use (your "brand").

As well, your place will also encompass other practitioners from whom you may receive referrals, and in turn, for you to refer to their specific areas of expertise. Being cognizant of the push and pull of both referrals and patient needs will also help define the way and location of what you decide to put down or locate.

## Promotion

While it is clear that lack of providers is endemic, and that patients will ultimately find providers who have availability, it is folly to not consider some sort of way to communicate your offerings and how they meet the needs of the market segment you are addressing. Depending on the product and the place, your ability to identify what *message* and *medium* you use will be a function of these factors.

Moreover, not only are the patients a key stakeholder, but also ancillary healthcare system members – hospitals, referring providers, physical/occupational therapists, rehabilitation centers, psychologists, visiting nurse associations, etc. – all need to know your offerings. Developing a promotional strategy, encompassing appropriate networking and advertising within channels used by these audiences, is an important component to consider when thinking about how your offering will be heard, seen, interpreted, and ultimately acquired. Again, thinking about the services you've used in your past experience guides you toward whom you need target as audiences for your advertising and networking efforts.

## Price

Much of what we do in the provider world is dictated by third-party payors, but that is no longer the only option available. The number of choices from monthly cash fees, to concierge medicine, to hybrid approaches have multiplied over the years. One of the most salient aspects of private practice today is the alternatives on how one can be compensated for the service being provided. The decision on this truly is one which can encompass all areas of medicine, whether primary care, specialty care, surgical care, or anything in between – we have seen cash only practices, to membership structures, to standard third-party payments – with examples of each from psychiatry to neurosurgery! Consideration of these types of options will be further described in later chapters, but thoughtful reflection on this in the planning stages would be wise.

## Financial Planning

You've now thought through what the product service is you will provide, and the patient type (market segment) you plan to approach. You've considered what utility you'll provide and bring to your patients, and any ancillary benefits. The how and where you will provide your service is something you've thought about as well, and finally how you'll get your name out there. Finally, you've thought about a model of compensation as well. And all of these areas will be covered again in ensuing chapters.

However, now that you've considered all of these things, you'll need to figure out (1) how much will it cost to start this endeavor, and (2) how much will it cost to operate the practice. This isn't something that is complicated but rather follows what you've already thought about with regard to your offering.

## Startup and Ongoing Expenses

There are many templates/lists out there to assess startup expenses; one example is in Table 3.1. Fundamentally these are expenses to start and run a business, which are common for us as providers.

**Table 3.1 Examples of Startup and Ongoing Expenses**

| |
|---|
| Permits and licenses – state license, city licenses for business |
| *Insurance – including malpractice, liability, benefit plans |
| Legal – business structure setup (e.g., limited liability corporation, LLC) |
| Marketing – vendor fees for social media, website, advertising; networking |
| *Office supplies – standard requirements |
| *Rental/lease – function of which model you plan to use |
| *Utilities – function of which model you plan to use |
| *Equipment – function of what area of medicine and offering you plan to provide; including computers and software, as well as an electronic medical record, phones, answering service (if needed), internet |
| Furniture/decor – function of what model you plan for your place |
| *Supplies – function of area of medicine and offering you plan to provide; estimate about three months of supplies initially |
| *Professional services – accounting/tax, marketing vendor, IT support, billing service, legal, insurance, customer relationship management/scheduling |
| *Payroll – provider, office manager, ancillary staff (e.g., nurse, medical assistant, reception) |
| *Loan payments – for initial startup costs and operations |

Note: * Ongoing expenses as well.

Now, based on experience and/or market expectations, create forecast on how much revenue you can plan per month. Many providers start creating a scheduling function to begin to book patients several weeks out BEFORE actually starting to see patients, in order to better provide both a more robust utilization of infrastructure at the start, and to better understand what revenues to expect. Notably, a key aspect of this is to ensure you have at least a handful of negotiated payment contracts with insurers BEFORE starting; otherwise, you'll be starting deep in the negative. It isn't recommended that you start out without this.

When creating this forecast, note also the "net" payment terms, or how long is the expectation of billing to receipt of funds. Once you have both startup expenses, ongoing expenses and revenue forecasts, you can calculate how long it will take to match revenues with expenses. By tallying revenues vs. expenses per month, you'll see when you break even and then when profitable; this will provide what initial capital will be required, from loans, people interested in investing in your practice, friends and family and other sources. Putting this on a spreadsheet with separate startup costs, then operating budget, will make it readable for interested parties, including yourself.

## Summary

If you've gone through this exercise, and completed each component and questions, you have written out a business plan. That wasn't so hard, now was it? Basically you've thought about what the need is, how you will satisfy it, your competitive advantage and why, and created a financial plan to make it happen. The epiphany is that this is pretty straightforward based on what you already know, and follows a logical progression thinking through what you can offer as a provider, and how you want to do it. You can certainly outsource this work to others, but only you know what you want to offer to patients who need you. A business plan template follows, which you can choose to use or find another that may match your style better. But again, by answering the questions above, you've written a plan.

This overview sets the stage for the details that follow in this book. But if you've gotten this far, you've done the lion's share of the work to set up a private practice *you want* – now it's about the details that we are here to guide you through.

## Business Plan Template

### Executive Summary

*Problem*: What problem needs to be solved (e.g., "There is a single Neurologist in the 1.2 million greater XXX area, with a wait for 12 months to be seen").

*Solution*: How will your offering create a solution (e.g., "NewNeuro plans to open an office which will service the southern half of the city with a demographic of X and a population of Y").

*Market:* Who will you target (e.g., "Our office will target those with outpatient neurologic needs, and those who require follow up after being in hospital X acutely").

*Competition*: Who is the competition? Who ISN'T the competition? (e.g., "There is a sole provider within the city who is booked out a year. While he also sees a similar demographic, the overall need is significant given the waiting time. We do not plan to compete with tele-medicine specialists on neurophysiologic studies, but rather will plan to have in-house services for the patients we see in our clinic").

*Why us:* The rationale for our competitive advantage (e.g., "NewNeuro will have state of the art and the most current treatments available for general neurologic diseases. We will be dedicated to providing high quality, prompt neurologic care to patients who currently wait up to a year to see a specialist")

**Overview**
Description of the patients, offerings, infrastructure anticipated, competition, startup/operating costs and anticipated revenues, and marketing overview from the answers to the questions in this chapter.

**Financing Need**
Amount required to finance startup/operations, with general use of funds (e.g., furniture, equipment, and licenses) and any other sources of funding anticipated from questions answered.

**Target Market**
Market segment description, how offering matches market segment, experience treating market segment, economic utility, benefits to the market segments as answered in the chapter questions.

**Keys to Success**
Identify specific aspects that are paramount to successful practice.
For example:

Third-party payment contracts obtained
Location
Staff
Expertise of provider, office manager, and accountant.
Unmet need to be fulfilled
New location in specific demographics (including patient access, access to referrals/hospital)
Marketing plan execution

**Execution**
*Marketing Plan*
Articulation of product, place, promotion and price.

*Operations Plan*
Articulation of third-party payment contracts obtained, customer relations management plan, and finance planning.

**Milestones**
Key aspects to be done.
For example:

Acquire third-party payment contracts – date
Acquire tranche of financing – date
Hire personnel – date
Hire vendors – date
Execute marketing plan – date
Start scheduling patients – date
Start seeing patients – date

**Anticipated Metrics**
Ways to measure growth of practice.
For example:

Revenues per month
New patients vs. return visits per month
Referrals in/out of practice
Social media "hits"
Acquisition of third-party payment contracts

**Practice Description**
Ownership/structure.
For example, sole proprietorship; LLC.

**Team**
Description of key personnel and leadership.
For example:
Provider, office manager, and support staff and background related to the practice of medicine

**Personnel Table with Salaries for Each Over Three-Year Period**
**Financial Plan**
Description in prose of the budget – for example, fee for service, cash basis, monthly recurring fees; ramp up of revenues/timing based on net-30/60/90 days; anticipated highest cost items and mitigation; ancillary activities to increase revenues (e.g., patient education sessions, clinical trials).

Formal budget with one year in monthly detail with figure showing revenues, expenses profit/loss, then ensuing two years quarterly.

**Financing**
**Use of Funds**
Articulation of funds usage including potential for cushion.

**Sources of Funds**
Articulation of loans, investors, friends/family, etc. and amounts

**Statements** (see Chapter 5):
**Balance Sheet**
**Income Statement**

# Chapter 4

# The Nuts and Bolts of Starting a Medical Practice

## Introduction

Creating a business starts with a great idea, and that's something that's certainly part of a medical practice. Your ability to offer a unique service to your community is what you bring to the table. In this chapter, we'll go over the aspects on developing your marketing plan (your "brand") to be able to promulgate the messages on your offering. There are other aspects to start the practice, which are the aspects that create the entity under which you're working. We call this the "nuts and bolts" aspect of starting a business, much of which you can do yourself, and other aspects for which you'll have to lean on brokers and your assembled team for help. Much of the setup occurs only once (as opposed to the cursed "modules" some of us have had to endure in corporate practice, which seem to be never ending). The addendum of this chapter has the checklist to help remind you of what needs to be done. Let's get started!

## Making It Legal

### *Structure*

The first thing you need to do to start the business is to create a business structure. While you can make a corporation, like an S- or C-corp, it's really not necessary, and a limited liability corporation (LLC) or professional LLC (PLLC) is fine to use. There's no significant difference between a PLLC and an LLC legally. The PLLC is most used by professionals, such as doctors, so that's what we would suggest since it's easy to create (*e.g.* Tom Crow MD PLLC). Although different business structures have their own advantages and disadvantages, a PLLC can usually be formed easily using online templates without requiring significant legal expertise. Even though it sounds like a corporation, PLLCs/LLCs are *not* incorporated (i.e., they're *companies*, not corporations), so no taxes


DOI: 10.4324/9781003685623-4

are paid individually as for a corporation like an S- or C-corp. You will file a component of your personal tax filings on the PLLC/LLC (schedule C).

### *Licenses to Do Business*

The next thing you need to do after forming the PLLC is to make sure it's registered, and you have the appropriate licenses in the location you want to practice. These are the business licenses needed for any business to start, and as usual, are associated with the locale charging the fees for you to be in business. These will be found on the city/county/state websites. In particular, virtually in every state, the Secretary of State requires you to set up an account with them to pay, as you would expect, state taxes, and if necessary, set up a state tax identification number. Not all states require the latter, but the Secretary of State office will let you know if that's necessary. So, each ".gov" site will let you know if you need a business license or not. For example, in the City of Colorado Springs, in El Paso County, Colorado, the state requires a registered LLC business license, but neither the city nor the county requires any additional documentation/licensing as of this writing. However, since you will be a physician, you are under DORA – the Department of Regulatory Affairs, which is associated with medical licensing; as you're no doubt aware, each state requires a license for you to practice medicine within its borders. But no issue there.

A word about the term "limited liability corporation". The owners of an LLC and PLLC are in general not *personally* responsible for the company's debts and liabilities, and as noted, have *pass through* taxation (schedule C, as noted). However, this structure does NOT prevent malpractice suits, therefore you need additional insurance for this and other liabilities (discussed later). Again, your legal counsel and insurance broker can be helpful in defining what your LLC covers.

## Money and People

### *Employer Identification Number*

Because you will be making money from the practice, taxes come into play. As a result, you need to have an *employer identification number* (EIN) from the IRS. This is pretty easy to obtain through the IRS.gov website, and as well can be done online when creating your PLLC. This will be the number that will be associated with the practice, which will be required for the business to do operations, from bank accounts (see below) to purchases of supplies, to tax filings. As noted by many others, it's essentially the social security number of the practice (same amount of numbers, but as opposed to 123-45-6789, it's 98-7654321). As noted, some states require a tax ID number as well, which you'll find on the state's website.

### *Your Team*

In general, the *starting* of the business requires a team that includes *legal*, *accounting*, and *tax* professionals. Each should have experience in small business services as well as medical practices. Since many of these providers also run small businesses, they can be of significant value particularly if sourced in the location in which you want to practice. We have had the experience of having service providers local in all of these areas with significant experience in domain knowledge of the area, to the best banks to use. Most of these professionals will provide some level of discount for a beginning business since they want to keep you as a client in the future (and be a referral source!).

Another group that you'll need going forward is different types of brokers, from real estate (if you're going to lease/rent/buy) to insurance. Again, using your network of providers (medical and nonmedical) will be helpful here. These providers also want to serve you well since you are a source of referrals in the future.

## Open a Business Bank Account

While it might be tempting to use your personal bank account for your business, *it's not wise to do so.* The accounting of cash flows as well as revenues and expenses will become *very* messy as a result, and the confusion and time it will take to audit the numbers (by you and your accountant) will cause you to want to tear your hair out! It's much better, and usually required, for you to have a separate bank account for the business. You want to keep your personal and business finances separate, and by keeping your business bank account under your PLLC, you garner the protection of that business structure. Most banks will have specific programs for small businesses, and they should be competing for your business. Recommendations from other doctors in the area are a good source of information, and the plethora of comparison websites for small business banking abound.

Here, you should be able to obtain advice from your chosen bank about the ways to accept payment. While the third-party payors (if you decide to accept insurance) will usually have a direct payment mechanism, it's important that you have a way to accept payments from patients (e.g., for cash pay patients, or to accept co-pays). Be sure to investigate and ask about the most technologically advanced payment systems, for example Zelle, Apple Pay, and Venmo – you want to be both convenient for people to pay you (of course!) *and* minimize the fees you pay (credit cards are notoriously expensive to accept!).

As an extension, while it may seem early to look into this, picking an accounting/payroll system up front is a key aspect when you're starting the business. You need to be familiar and facile with its mechanisms, so pick a system with which you can work. As well, be sure the program can be contoured to professional offices, and one which your accountant can work with. There are systems that also integrate with cloud computing for backup and security, and others that can interface with your practice bank account. At a minimum, we suggest choosing a system that allows you to see the revenues and costs easily, that can be backed up to a cloud server, and that your accountant can access and interpret with you. Your accountant and the Small Business Administration (SBA) can be helpful in this regard.

## Protect Yourself: Insurance

Business insurance, along with malpractice insurance, is required for your business and yourself. You need to protect the practice and yourself against various aspects over which you have limited control. One or more insurance brokers will be required for this – interestingly, one of us had a real estate broker who was a huge source of other excellent brokers for insurance of various types. While there are specific requirements from loan sources (see Chapter 5) to business requirements to regulatory needs (see Chapter 12), you should not skimp on insurance; it adds piece of mind to known, and more importantly unknown risks, for you and your practice. This includes the following:

1. *Health insurance*: Whether you do this as a group insurance, or individual insurance where the practice picks up part of the tab should be assessed based on cost.
2. *Property insurance:* If you've decided to hold onto things like inventory and clinical supplies, this is needed to cover any losses.

3. *Comprehensive general liability (CGL)*: This is insurance covering you from injury suffered by visitors to your business. Second, should you get sued, CGL covers the cost of your defense on this basis (not malpractice).
4. *Business interruption*: This covers losses from an inability to conduct business due to fire, flood, and disaster.
5. *Malpractice*: We cover malpractice insurance in another (entire) chapter (Chapter 12). This can also include errors and omissions and product liability insurance.
6. *Workers' compensation*: If you have employees, you will be required to carry workers' compensation insurance for work-related injuries.
7. *Disability*: Disability insurance covers you when you can't work because you are disabled due to injury.

There are other types of insurance such as umbrella insurance and key person insurance which can also be obtained; there may be state requirements as well, which can be found on the state government's website and can be identified by your broker.

## Trademarks, Copyright, and/or Patents

Another aspect that arises is protection of your (and in turn, your practice's) intellectual property. Perhaps you've come up with a procedure you use in the OR that has created great results; maybe you've found a way to sequence medication for better outcomes in patients with diabetes; still further, maybe you've created a new technology that seems to be better than whatever is out there. That's all potentially patentable, and you should consult a patent agent to see if it's something that you should be protecting.

In addition, you may be a writer of blogs, articles, or other aspects; be sure that you protect yourself with copyright since that may also be a source of revenues in the future. The key is that your intellectual property may expand beyond what you may consider, so always talk to agents who are familiar with these aspects. Your lawyer can help identify appropriate agents.

We cover branding in Chapter 6, but you should start considering what type of symbol and catch phrases you want to have associated with the practice. A brand is a representation of you and your practice, and it should be minimally trademarked for you and your practice's sole use; similarly, having a brand statement should be trademarked as well, if possible. These are the representations of your reputation and what you want patients to recall when they think about the practice, so choosing something appropriately memorable is important!

## Hiring

If you plan to run your practice entirely solo, you can skip this section. However, while the broad term of hiring can include the service providers as noted for your team, what we're talking about here is an employee or employees to help in the tasks of the practice. Mostly, our suggestion is to have a specific *process* to bringing someone on board. This includes a job description, pay scale (developed through your research and budgeting), how you plan to assess (who will interview, how many references, doing a background check), assessment of cost of benefits (again, in your budget), and a real understanding of what you need at this stage of the practice. Looking for experiences from other practitioners who started practices is helpful with the latter. The relevant point is making sure you have a process that helps guide you to getting the person you want. A personal piece of advice is, "hire character; train skill" – our (and other's) collective experience has seen this to be the most important aspect of creating a thriving work environment; having high level of expertise and poor attitude will detract from your most valuable resource, viz., your time. This will be discussed further in the chapter on staffing.

Similarly, have a book of standard operating procedures (SOP) for the practice. This protects you and sets expectations of the staff (if any) for what you expect for an employment environment. You don't want to have an employee claim that there was no guidance on spending three hours on lunch since there was no SOP manual. Consultants for practices as well as your legal counsel can provide you templates that you can adopt or pay someone to adopt to your own needs.

## Starting Points

The nuts and bolts of starting a business would be incomplete if we did not cover the cost-containment mindset, and what it entails. The key to being a good practice is to be able to control costs while continuing to provide your services to the community. Our perspective having managed our own "P&L" (profit and loss statement – see Finance chapter) is that not only is it doable, but you also have the flexibility to create value and prioritize to maximize what's important to you, whether that be revenues or taking time off every Friday or Wednesday. So, let's cover some overarching concepts of the practice and management of it.

1. Start small: While your plans of being a super subspecialist in a large urban area may be totally realistic, growing into your practice ensures your vision doesn't outpace your revenues. It's like your household – don't buy that huge mansion quite yet, or that Escalade, when you're just starting out. You'll have time later on if you decide that's what you need (often we understand later these things aren't necessary!).
2. Be relentless with costs: Scrutinize the expenses you have and ensure that you are getting both the best deal, and that whatever you're spending money on, it's for the right reason. Just because you can amortize or deduct something off your taxes does not mean it's a no brainer – do you really need that super-de-duper 16-sample centrifuge? Or does your current standard eight tube one work just fine? Do you need an answering service, or can you use e-paging to covering physicians? Be ready to look at your revenues/costs weekly, and your collections at least monthly to see the revenue stream and cost centers. Knowledge is power, if you need to do something about either.
3. Be realistic about bringing people on: People are the most expensive part of any business. They cost you training time (but be ready to do so – remember, hire for personality, train for skills), salary, and benefits (if you decide to give them). They also need to be managed by you. This also goes not only for staff, but for clinical people like physician assistants and nurses. Be very, very sure you want to add that expense if you haven't done your homework on the profitability of these personnel. Your budget and finance calculations will help.
4. Understand what you get paid for, *and what you don't*: We have advised that you pre-schedule patients before the start of the practice, as well as negotiate to have payor contracts in place when you start. However, you will need to keep an eye out on payment times, as well as amounts, of these contracts; if they are too cumbersome and cost you too much time, you have to look to change the terms or the number of patients you see (see Chapter 9). Further, you have to see what the payors/patients are paying you for and prioritize those activities; if

they're not paying you for answering an email, deprioritize or delegate that function; if they are paying you for a given procedure that you do, ensure you keep that in mind when looking at the list of things you need to do. Knowing where your revenues come from (and where they don't) will help you run your business efficiently, prioritizing those activities that are value-added – and what patients are.

5. Be diligent about time: Whether this is the amount of time per patient, time you spend in meetings, time you allow for tasks to be done, it's your most valuable resource. It's also one that you have control over, and why you went into private practice in the first place!

## Checklist and Timeline

At the end of this chapter, we include a checklist and timeline for starting the practice. The ensuing chapters will cover many aspects that are in the timeline; we've tried to cover the preparation work in this chapter so that you can start the process and obtain the right help for getting your practice off the ground quickly and with momentum! Importantly, once much of this is set up, the hard work is done, and it's monitoring and/or your brokers who are helping you with tasks. When you've done the preparation work, you can start with the timeline herein – this is just an example, and you can speed it up or slow it down as needed for your practice. Included as well is a trial run – this is strongly suggested as a "time out" to be sure everything is in place, by running through scheduling, what happens when a patient comes through the door, is seen by the staff/provider, from check in to check out. While we may not foresee every bump in the road, it will allow you to see the major ones and correct them before you start seeing "real" patients.

## Checklist for Preparation for a New Practice: What's Needed on a "Nuts and Bolts" Level

There are services that will help set up all of the following as "business formation provider". Just make sure *all* of these are completed.

- Legally form your business: Determine the type of business structure (usually an LLC, or professional LLC, PLLC, which is what many doctors use).
- For the location you pick, check the city/county/state registration requirements and go to the secretary of state website of the business location to establish an account (alas, you have to pay taxes)
- Obtain city/county/state licenses to open a business and practice
- Obtain an EIN from the IRS (again, for tax purposes). This can be done easily online or when you set up the PLLC/LLC. You'll have to have the name of your practice through the PLLC/LLC (e.g., Josephine Smithereens MD PLLC).
- Open a business bank account. Do NOT use your personal bank account or merge the accounts; it will make your accounting far more difficult going forward. As well, legal separation is important with regard to liability. Be sure the bank you choose understands the type of business you're running (i.e., not a new airplane manufacturing plant, but a small business).
- Identify your team: Legal, tax, accountant – all can help with the start-up paperwork and give breaks for new businesses. Use either your network, other doctors you've worked with, or local professional agencies to identify good people with whom to work.

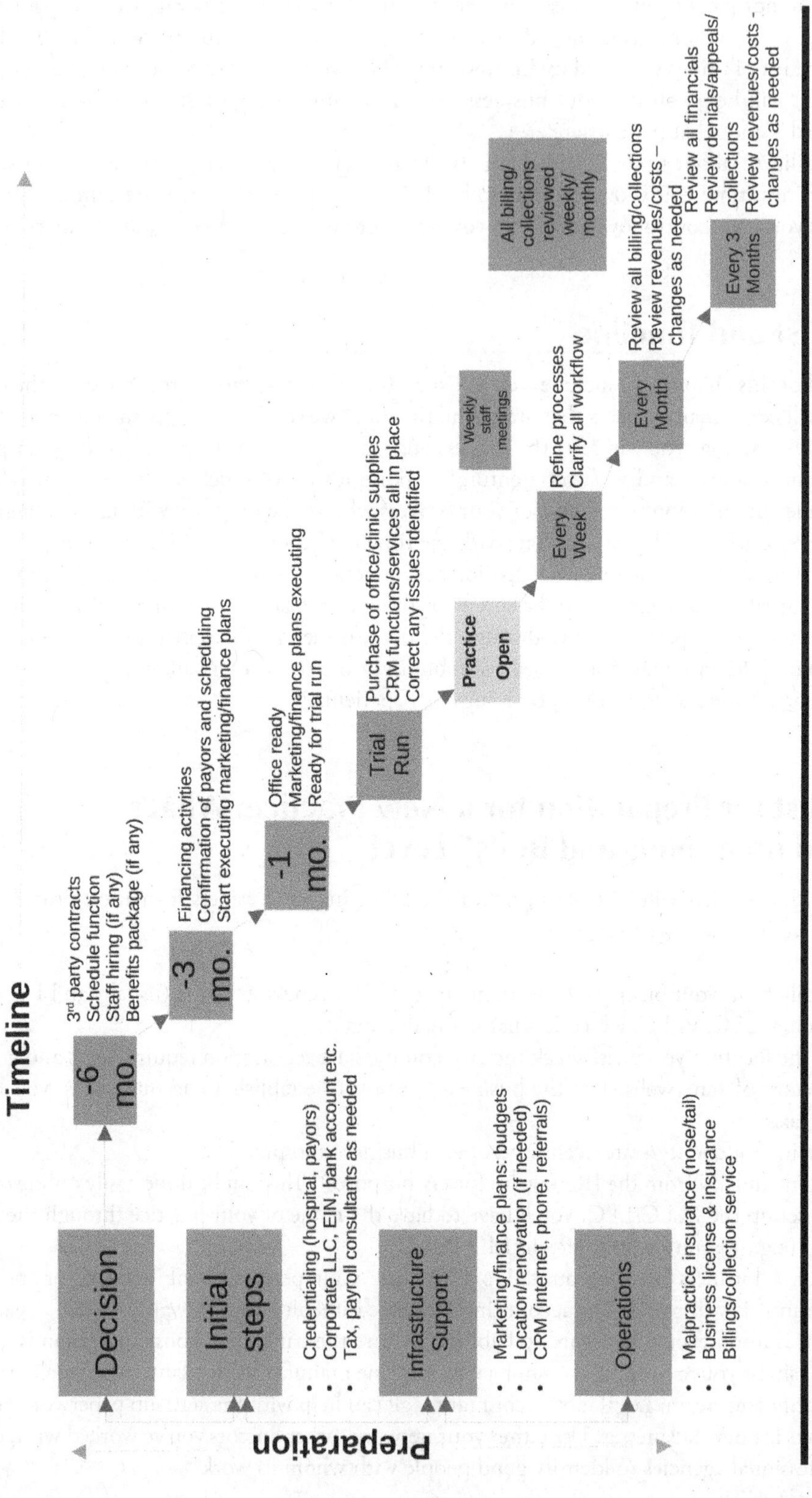
Timeline
Preparation
Decision
Initial steps
Credentialing (hospital, payors)
Corporate LLC, EIN, bank account etc.
Tax, payroll consultants as needed
Infrastructure Support
Marketing/finance plans: budgets
Location/renovation (if needed)
CRM (internet, phone, referrals)
Operations
Malpractice insurance (nose/tail)
Business license & insurance
Billings/collection service
-6 mo.
3rd party contracts
Schedule function
Staff hiring (if any)
Benefits package (if any)
-3 mo.
Financing activities
Confirmation of payors and scheduling
Start executing marketing/finance plans
-1 mo.
Office ready
Marketing/finance plans executing
Ready for trial run
Trial Run
Purchase of office/clinic supplies
CRM functions/services all in place
Correct any issues identified
Practice Open
Every Week
Refine processes
Clarify all workflow
Weekly staff meetings
Every Month
Review all billing/collections
Review revenues/costs – changes as needed
All billing/ collections reviewed weekly/ monthly
Every 3 Months
Review all financials
Review denials/appeals/ collections
Review revenues/costs - changes as needed

**Figure 4.1**

- Pick a reliable accounting system your accountant is familiar with, and matches the needs of your business. There are programs that are made for professional offices like yours, but general software can also be used easily. Our recommendations are to have a system that you feel comfortable using to assess revenues/costs, that can be tied to your banking software, and which can be cloud-based for security and back up purposes.
- Ensure you have adequate insurance: This is business insurance, rather than (just) malpractice insurance. You should of course have malpractice insurance, and we've dedicated an entire chapter to that. Here, we're talking about the insurance to run a business. Again, you'll need a broker for these types of policies. As noted in the chapter, this includes:
  1. *Health insurance*: Whether you do this as a group insurance or individual insurance where the practice picks up part of the tab should be assessed based on cost.
  2. *Property insurance*: If you've decided to hold onto things like inventory and clinical supplies, this is needed to cover any losses.
  3. *CGL*: This is insurance covering you from injury suffered by visitors to your business. Second, should you get sued, CGL covers the cost of your defense on this basis (not malpractice).
  4. *Business interruption*: This covers losses from an inability to conduct business due to fire, flood, and disaster.
  5. *Malpractice*: We cover malpractice insurance in an entire chapter. This can also include errors and omissions and product liability insurance.
  6. *Workers' compensation*: If you have employees, this will be required to carry workers' compensation insurance for work-related injuries.
  7. *Disability*: Disability insurance covers you when you can't work because you are disabled due to injury.
- Protect your brand with trademarks, copyright, and/or patents. Your lawyer can help with this.
- Ensure you have systems to take payments from not only insurers but patients as well (e.g., co-pays). Credit card systems are usual, but being able to take cash, checks, and electronic payments (e.g., Zelle, Apple Pay, and Venmo) is a good idea.
- Have a process for any hiring you plan to do. Your assembled team can help you with this.
- Create/purchase a set of SOP. For a practice, you want to have something that targets your type of business. Your legal advisor as well as any business consultant can help with this aspect.

# Chapter 5

# Finance

## Introduction

Most providers are familiar with budgeting, whether from personal experience or that which has been associated with other professional duties. However, many have had little exposure to the more detailed intricacies of the more nuanced aspects of finance, which is not surprising given the emphasis on other aspects during undergraduate and medical training.

The term "finance" can strike a chord of fear and loathing within our ranks. However, it is, like any area of medicine, just another set of vocabulary within which we can understand another system. It acts to summarize our activities, either from a look historically or into the future for planning purposes, similar to a past medical history and assessment and plan, respectively. If you can manage the cash in your wallet and your credit card bills, finance is straightforward since that's all we're doing.

This chapter's purpose is thus to provide an overview to the provider of the finance area, and how it is used to help understand how your practice is running, as well as how your practice can allocate resources and determine if these decisions are effecting their intended goal. To be clear, it's NOT to become an accountant (you should hire someone to do that function); rather, it is the ability to read an income statement, a balance sheet, and a cash flow assessment toward understanding your practice's financial health, which is the goal. So, let's get started.

## Types of Accounting

Fundamentally, there are two types of accounting. The first is financial accounting, which is a measure on how an entity (e.g., your practice) has performed during a defined time period. It's a *historical evaluation* based on a given set of rules; you may have heard in the media discussions of "GAAP accounting" (generally accepted accounting principles) that govern the reporting of companies.


DOI: 10.4324/9781003685623-5

While your practice need not incorporate all those rules, in general, financial accounting lets you see your practice's past history of performance.

The second type of accounting is managerial finance. This is used to provide information about where expenses and revenues are arising and has maximal flexibility to be tailored to evaluate options for your practice. It is thus more *focused on the future* and collects information from different departments to evaluate alternatives and constraints by which the practice can plot a future direction and strategy. One can consider it a forward-looking function for decision-making.

You can use both types of accounting to help manage your practice. We will focus on the financial statements of the *balance sheet, the cash flow statement and the income statement* as the verbiage for the state of health of your practice.

## Data Format

### *The Balance Sheet*

The balance sheet is a snapshot in time of your practice and describes the assets (what the practice has that holds value) and liabilities (that which is owed or will be owed to others) at a specific time. The key concept here is the assets and liabilities must always match, that is, "balance". Some key definitions are given in the following:

*Assets*: That which a company owns or has claim to; assets can be represented by the formula: assets = liabilities + shareholder equity.

*Liabilities*: A company's obligations to pay or deliver something of value in the future.

Adding the term "current" to each of the above (arbitrarily) indicates that which can be turned into cash (assets) or must be paid (liabilities) within one year.

*Payables*: Money owed to parties outside the company.

*Receivables*: Money owed from parties outside the company.

*Shareholder equity*: The assets of the company minus the liabilities (viz., what the company owns subtracted by what the company owes, by definition); this tends to be a challenging concept for some, but it is just the accounting or "book" estimate of the shareholder value of investment in the entity (practice).

Note that shareholder equity may bear little or no relationship to the market value of the equity of the practice. For example, a successful practice that has built up a large patient base early on but still owes startup capital to a bank may have a relatively small shareholder equity, or "book value" due to initial accumulated borrowing/losses, but have large market value due to the anticipation of the practice's ability to generate value (revenue).

*Depreciation*: A method showing how much of an asset's life is "used up"; in financial accounting terms, allocating the cost of an asset over its useful life.

Let's look at a balance sheet of a hypothetical practice.

Table 5.1 shows Balance sheet PracticeCo, yearend 20XX.

Note all transactions within the balance sheet always have a "double entry" to keep both sides equal. This is a key rule of financial accounting; any transaction whether increasing assets (e.g., purchasing a $1000 piece of equipment, where property, plant, and equipment (PP&E) will increase

**Table 5.1 Balance Sheet, PracticeCo, End of Year 20XX**

| **Assets** | | **Liabilities and Shareholder Equity** | |
|---|---|---|---|
| *Current assets:* | | *Current liabilities:* | |
| Cash | 10,000 | Accounts payable | 2000 |
| Accounts receivable | 9000 | Income tax payable | 4000 |
| Inventory | 500 | | |
| *Total current assets* | 19,500 | *Total current liabilities* | 6000 |
| | | Long-term debt | 500 |
| | | Other long-term liabilities | 500 |
| | | Long term liabilities | 1000 |
| | | Total liabilities | 7000 |
| *Fixed assets:* Land | 30,000 | *Shareholder equity:* | |
| Property, plant, equipment | 100,000 | Common stock | 54,000 |
| Accumulated depreciation | –50,000 | Retained earnings | 37,500 |
| *Total fixed assets* | 80,000 | *Total shareholder equity* | 92,500 |
| **Total assets** | 99,500 | **Total liabilities and Shareholder equity** | 99,500 |

Note: Underlined values are sums from values above resultant in values below.

by $1000, shareholder equity will decrease by $1000) or taking out an $10,000 loan (where cash will increase by $10,000, and debt/liabilities will increase by the same) to keep a balance. To emphasize: this is to show the practice's financial picture at a moment in time (typically at the end of an accounting period, such as a quarter or fiscal year).

So, to recap: the balance sheet reflects the state of the practice at a moment in time; assets and liabilities/shareholder equity "balance" at all times, whether within an end of year statement, or when any transaction occurs. All of accounting follows the formula: Assets = liabilities + shareholder equity.

## The Income Statement

The income statement (also known as the profit and loss statement, or "P&L") is a key aspect as it shows what revenues were brought into the company over a particular time period (rather than a specific moment in time like the balance sheet). This data thus represents a way to look at the operations of the practice, described as profits and/or income. Some additional definitions to aid in the discussion:

*Net sales:* Revenues obtained from sales efforts minus any returned items or discounts (such as Medicare rebates for drugs).

*Cost of goods sold (COGS)*: Overall costs for the sold product, including such things as the cost of the materials used in creating the product, along with direct labor costs and manufacturing overhead; however, it does NOT include the indirect expenses such as distribution costs, sales force costs, laboratory costs, research personnel costs, insurance costs, or other administrative overhead costs.

**Table 5.2 Income Statement for PracticeCo**

| | *20XX* |
|---|---|
| Net revenues/sales | 26,000 |
| Cost of goods sold | 14,000 |
| **Gross profit** | 12,000 |
| Selling, general, and administrative expenses | 3500 |
| Research and development expenses | 2200 |
| Office expenses | 300 |
| *Total operating expenses* | 6000 |
| **Operating income** | 6000 |
| Interest expense | 555 |
| Other nonoperating expenses (e.g., renovations) | 200 |
| *Total nonoperating expenses* | 755 |
| Income before taxes | 5,245 |
| Provision for income taxes | 1,980 |
| **Net income** | 3,265 |

*Selling, general and administrative expenses (SG&A)*: This typically includes the selling expenses of the sales force, marketing expenses, management personnel costs, as well as general and administrative expenses that the firm expends.

*Amortization:* The paying off of debt by regular installments.

*The income statement ties back to the balance sheet via the net income produced.* This is seen on the balance sheet as changes in retained earnings. There is a direct relationship between the income statement and the equity part of the balance sheet; any net income obtained from operations of the practice creates wealth ("value") for those who have "invested" in the practice, manifest as equity. The converse, of course, is also true; any losses due to operations destroy wealth for those investing in the company, but we are hopeful this is not the outcome!

Table 5.2 is an example of the income statement for PracticeCo.

To recap: the income statement reflects a time period (as opposed to a moment in time) describing revenues generated by operations. Profitability results from having net revenues exceed expenses. The income statement is linked to the balance sheet by the generation of net income that flows into retained earnings.

## The Cash Flow Statement

This statement *documents the sources and uses of cash within the practice, and is the most relevant operational metric in finance*. Like the income statement, it is defined over a period of time to reflect the operations of the practice. However, the focus of the cash flow statement is to determine whether sufficient cash is being generated by operations of the practice to pay both the operating and capital (e.g., loan) expenses. Obviously, if a practice doesn't generate sufficient cash, starting cash or cash

**Table 5.3 Cash Flow Statement for PracticeCo for Year 20XX**

| *Cash* | *20XX* |
|---|---|
| Cash flow from operating activities: | |
| Net income | 3,265 |
| Adjustments to net income from operations: | |
| Depreciation and amortization | 2200 |
| Other noncash expenses (e.g., fuel) | 200 |
| Changes in assets and liabilities: | |
| Increase in inventory | 11 |
| Increase in accounts receivable | –3 |
| Increase in accounts payable | –4 |
| **Net cash provided by operations** | 5669 |
| Cash flows from investing: | |
| Capital expenditures | –12 |
| Sale of property, plant, equipment | 2 |
| **Net cash provided by investing** | –10 |
| Cash flows from financing activities: | |
| Increase in borrowing | 19 |
| Dividends paid | 0 |
| Exchange rate changes | 0 |
| **Net cash provided from financing activities** | 19 |
| **Net increase (decrease) in cash** | 5,678 |

generated from sale of assets on the balance sheet will be used to fund expenses. If internal cash (e.g., retained earnings) is insufficient, external financing (e.g., from debt or equity) will be required. Thus, when looking at the cash flow statement, one needs to be cognizant of cash obtained from operations, investment, and financing. *Generally, most cash flow statements look at the beginning of a time period compared to the end of a time period.*

Table 5.3 is an example of PracticeCo's cash flow statement.

In this example, we can see the importance of cash payments. An increase in the accounts receivable (i.e., another party owes the practice, but has not paid as of yet) is NOT a cash payment, but rather a USE OF CASH (credit). In contrast, in the income statement this is considered revenue. In addition, an increase in accounts payable actually increases cash (albeit somewhat counterintuitive – however, cash will ultimately decrease once a payable is actually paid).

The effect of depreciation is also seen here. This affects both the income statement and the cash flow statement. For the former, it decreases the net income of the practice and thus decreases the overall taxes the practice needs to pay. However, for the latter, it increases the cash flow, since depreciation is not cash, but "use" of assets, and hence it is NOT a cash charge. Further, payments are either *expensed* (as expenses on the cash flow statement) or *capitalized* (included as a capital expenditure on the cash flow statement), which in turn are linked to the long-term assets on the end of period balance sheet. Long-term assets are then depreciated over their useful life (for the most part). This links all the data descriptors on the finance side. The latter is important for practice managers/

providers, as purchases of equipment are generally treated as capital expenditures and NOT immediately expensed.

Hence, a final recap: while the interpretations of the balance sheet, income statement, and cash flow statements can be further analyzed, this general overview allows for an understanding of the health of a practice – *it's expenditures, revenues, cash flow for and from operations* – whether it is creating value (making money) or losing value.

## Interpreting Data: Use of Ratios

The use of ratios can help those directing a practice to compare data from a year/years to understand financial performance. In particular, ratios can help with comparing different approaches (strategies) used over time to assess the financial performance of the practice. With the data from the balance sheet, income statement, and cash flow statement, ratios can be derived that can help determine the relative health of the practice. We'll use PracticeCo's statements to assess the financial performance ratios.

## Financial Ratios

### *Return on Equity (ROE)*

This is probably the most used evaluation of past performance.

ROE = net income/shareholder equity

= 3265/93500 = 3.5%

In other words, for every dollar of shareholder investment, the practice earns $.035 of profit. In general, this is something we compare over time periods to ensure we're increasing our ROE.

### *Return on Assets (ROA)*

This is a manifestation of both the profit margin and asset turnover; it is how efficiently the assets are being used to generate profit.

ROA = net income/assets

= 3265/99500 = 3.3% or $.033.

PracticeCo earned 3.3 cents profit for every dollar in assets. As per the ROE, we look at this over time to be sure our practice is increasing in returns per assets.

## Liquidity Ratios

The term "liquidity" represents the ability of the practice to generate cash from its assets, and thus is a short-term assessment. It is important to understand the relevance of these ratios since vendors and creditors will use such ratios to evaluate the relative level/ability to pay short-term obligations (e.g., loans).

### *Working Capital (WC)*

This provides vendors/creditors or anyone interested in investing in the practice an understanding of the operating efficiency (viz., the short-term financial health). Typically, a positive value indicates the ability to pay off short-term obligations (debt and liabilities). Somewhat counterintuitive is that money tied up in inventory (less relevant) and money owed to the practice (more relevant – accounts receivable) *increase* WC.

WC = current assets – current liabilities

= 19,500 – 6000 = 13,500.

Thus, PracticeCo has a positive WC and would be expected to be able to pay off current obligations.

## Current Ratio (CR)

This is another way to evaluate whether the practice has the ability to pay off short-term obligations. A value at least greater than one and preferably higher suggests practice ability to pay debt and liabilities.

CR = current assets/current liabilities

= 19,500/6000 = 3.25

PracticeCo has a relatively strong CR.

## Leverage Ratios

Leverage is the use of debt. Debt financing creates an obligation and recurrent expense (including interest) but adds revenue without diluting shareholder equity. Interest is an expense, and evaluating leverage in a practice revolves around using a cash flow measure to determine if there is sufficient amounts to service debt payments.

## Debt-to-Equity Ratio

A common measure of financial leverage – this measures the solvency based on how much debt is being used in the practice's capital structure.

Debt-to-equity ratio = total debt (both short and long term)/shareholder equity

= 500/93,500 = 0.5%

This indicates for every dollar supplied by shareholders, \$.005 is being supplied by creditors, indicating a very low degree of leverage for the practice. The use of debt varies from practice to practice;

**Table 5.4 Ratios Used in Financial Analysis Financial Performance**

| | |
|---|---|
| Return on equity (ROE) = Net income/ shareholder equity | Shows generation of income per amount invested by shareholders. Typically compared over time periods. |
| Return on assets (ROA) = Net income/ assets | Documents generation of income per amount of assets in the practice. As per ROE, typically compared over time periods. |
| Working capital (WC) = Current assets – current liabilities | The ability to pay off short-term ("current") obligations (debt) |
| Current ratio (CR) = Current assets/ current liabilities | Another assessment of ability to meet short-term obligations similar to WC |
| Debt-to-equity ratio = Total debt/ shareholder equity | Shows how much debt is being used in the practice; one typically wants to minimize debt unless determining whether an investment is warranted |

again, comparing this over time to ensure leverage being used is overall minimized (unless making an investment – see NPV below).

A summary of ratios is used in Table 5.4.

## Discounted Cash Flow

So, to this point, we have covered how to evaluate the practice at a point in time (balance sheet), over a period of time (income statement), and from one point in time to another (cash flow statement), as well as a combination of both (ratios). These provide a background for which decisions can be made about what direction or changes might be made to alter components of the practice to create more value (or to keep things the way they are).

However, when changes are desired, a metric needs to be evaluated to determine whether such "investment" of resources would be expected to return better returns than just putting money in the bank and collecting (low) interest. To be clear, there needs to be an expectation that the practice will benefit in some manner (however defined – revenues, reputation, market access, etc.) in the future with the investment.

As well, this emphasizes something we are all taught (but often forget), viz., *the time value of money*. A dollar today is worth more than a dollar obtained at some time in the future. This further articulates that cash flow is the MOST relevant aspect in finance; while accounting treatments are important, they are backward looking and do not describe the future ability to generate cash. *As a result, any investment in a project or program by the practice manager/provider must be analyzed by what cash value is anticipated for the future, discounted back to the present compared to any outlay of capital.* This process is known as *discounted cash flow analysis*, and many have heard of the terms associated with it (see below) but have limited exposure on how it is actually calculated. However, this is the basis by which decisions can be made on whether an investment should be made going forward for the practice. Let's look at the most common ones used, net present value (NPV) and internal rate of return (IRR).

## Net Present Value

This is probably the most used financial valuation calculation, and most have at least heard the term. The NPV method of project valuation uses a discount rate ("cost of capital" – the return that could be obtained by the practice by investing elsewhere) to calculate the value of the project. It can also be considered the ***opportunity cost*** – that is, the cost to do this project vs. another.

NPV = present value of future cash inflows – initial investment

Note that the dollars used in this equation are today's dollars. When an NPV is positive, it suggests that the investment in the project is exceeded by a return greater than the cost of capital and suggests a project should go forward since it will increase the wealth of the practice. When NPV is negative, it is apparent the opposite is true; the project is costing more than that cost of capital and should be rejected. Finally, if the NPV is zero, the project is the same as the cost of capital, and other factors should be evaluated on whether such a project should be done (e.g., increased reputation of the practice and opportunity cost to staff).

A word on the cost of capital, viz., discount rate. This is the opportunity cost a practice incurs by investing in a project vs. an alternative similar risk investment. While there are sophisticated ways to calculate a cost of capital, it is generally a risk-free interest rate + risk premium (the reward any investor would expect/demand for a perceived level of risk). To simplify, often used with a US government bond (three-month T-bill) + average earned in the public equity markets. Historically, the former is about 3–4%; the latter 5–6%, and thus the range could be 8–10%.

In practice, the NPV looks at revenues over a time period vs. costs at a given cost of capital. The fortunate aspect is that most spreadsheets have a function to allow for calculation by inputting the costs, discount rate, and anticipated revenues.

## Internal Rate of Return

An alternative of the NPV, the IRR represents the discount rate equal to the present value of the cash going into the project; this is the discount rate when the NPV = 0. This is particularly useful to calculate when cash inflows are different from time period to time period. The calculation is not as straightforward as the NPV, but can in general be done with spreadsheets as per the NPV. The general rule is a project where the IRR is greater than the discount rate should be funded, and conversely, one where the IRR is less should not be. IRR does not consider the cost of capital, which is another advantage, since the latter can be different during different parts of the project, and thus multiple IRRs can be associated with a project. However, in general, with defining assumptions, the NPV can provide a similar answer on going forward with a project, and thus since it does take into account cost of capital, is a preferred method for general use.

So, in general, the ability to generate cash from operations is the primary concern of the practice manager/provider. NPV requires forecasts of initial capital required, and anticipated future cash flows for projects under consideration, as well as the discount rate applied; an NPV > 0 suggests a firm should invest in a project; NPV < 0 suggests rejection of a project; NPV = 0 requires further evaluation. NPV can be used to both determine wealth creation for a company as well as prioritization of projects/programs for a firm. IRR represents the discount rate where the NPV = 0. The NPV provides clearer information for most situations than the IRR and is preferred in most value calculations, at least from a theoretical point of view.

## Glossary

**Amortization**: The paying off of debt by regular installments.

**Assets**: That which a company owns or has claim to.

**Common stock**: Representation of ownership.

**Cost of goods sold (COGS):** Overall costs for the sold product, including such things as the cost of the materials used in creating the product, along with direct labor costs and manufacturing overhead; however, it does NOT include the indirect expenses such as distribution costs, sales force costs, laboratory costs, research personnel costs, insurance costs, or other administrative overhead costs.

**Leverage**: Use of debt to fund operations.

**Liabilities**: A company's obligations to pay or deliver something of value.

**Liquidity**: The ability to generate cash from assets.

**Net sales**: Revenues obtained from sales efforts minus any returned items or discounts (such as Medicare rebates for drugs). It does NOT include the indirect expenses such as distribution costs, sales force costs, laboratory costs, research personnel costs, insurance costs, or other administrative overhead costs.

**Payables**: Money owed to parties outside the company.

**Property, plant, equipment**: Tangible, long-term assets (also known as fixed assets).

**Receivables**: Money owed from parties outside the company.

**Retained earnings**: Accumulated net income that is retained at a given point in time,

**Selling, general and administrative expenses (SG&A):** This typically includes the selling expenses of the sales force, marketing expenses, management personnel costs, as well as general and administrative expenses.

**Shareholder equity**: The assets of the company minus the liabilities.

# Chapter 6

# Marketing

## Introduction

In Chapters 3 and 4 we showed how thinking about your expertise and your experience with previous patients gives you a fundamental and strong basis for your practice as you move forward. You've already created the foundation of a marketing plan, by considering what makes you unique and what types of things you offer that the competition does not. You have also already thought about the market segment (patients) you wish to serve, the size of the market, how patients will access your practice (and how you might let them know about the practice), and how you will measure what success means to you.

Further, you are able to describe what your potential patients want, as well as how you might be able to match your location, your time available, and the various detailed offerings you will have to provide to the patients. In this chapter, we'll dive more into the marketing plan, explaining the practical aspects of each component and how it applies to a new practice; this is focused on the patient first, and how the practice can access these patients. By using what you've done earlier, and developing it further with the details herein, you'll have your marketing plan ready for execution. Write out each of these details for your plan!

## Market Segmentation

In Chapter 3, we defined a market as a group of customers who are seeking a particular service. For you, this is a set of patients that have a *medical need*, which is currently unsatisfied and that your competitive advantage can fulfill. These patients have the resources to "transact" (i.e., visit your office and obtain services from you). This constitutes a market segment, and in your case, a *patient population*, since we're looking at the benefits the patients receive from your services. Nonetheless, we'll use the terms interchangeably.


DOI: 10.4324/9781003685623-6

Now, as part of the exercise, you need to understand that there are different parts of a market, and there are aspects that are more attractive to pursue. This is part of the *size* of the market, one which you can target with your marketing effort. Indeed, by identifying a more homogenous and more focused mix, you have a higher chance of success to be able to deliver a resounding message that will prompt patients to access your services. This is important since it is virtually impossible to market to every potential customer using mass approaches – the amount of resources required would be Herculean wiping out any return on investment. Thus, the time spent on identifying the types of patients you want to serve, viz., through the initial effort of evaluating adequate size, accessibility, measurability, and ability to respond to a reasonably sized marketing plan, is the first key step in your practice. The great thing is, if you've done the exercise previously, you've done this already!

## Economic Utility

We previously spoke about economic utility. There are four types of economic utility we address: form, place, time, and information utility. So why are these relevant? Because these details form the basis by which you will create your offering for the patients you wish to serve and hence market to; *it's the value your patients assign to your practice in satisfying their unmet medical need.*

## Form Utility

To review, form utility refers to the services that you will provide to your patients. Marketing supports form utility by communicating the needs of patients to the provider/s of the practice and *vice versa. By evaluating the marketplace by the characteristics in Tables 6.1 and 6.2, you have effectively addressed form utility in your assessment.* Sometimes you have to modify your form utility when you

**Table 6.1 Components of Market Segmentation**

| |
|---|
| **Adequate size:** Patient numbers must be large enough so providing services in this marketplace is profitable |
| **Accessibility:** Patients should be targetable with reasonable marketing activities |
| **Measurability:** Market potential should be measurable by numbers of patients and reimbursement (e.g., not just Medicare) |
| **Response to marketing mix:** Patients are expected to respond to your unique marketing mix favorably |

**Table 6.2 Examples of Characteristics Used to Create Market/Customer (Patient) Segmentation**

| |
|---|
| **Demographics** Age, Sex, Marital Status |
| **Income level** High, Middle Low |
| **Type of insurance** Levels of profitability |
| **Lifestyle activities, interests** |
| **Geographic zip code and transport logistics** |
| **Usage patterns** Frequency, severity of disease, reliability of follow-up |
| **Other benefits needed** Primary vs. specialty care |

obtain feedback from your patients; one of us was initially seeing oncology patients, and when a patient came to the office with a different diagnosis, they mentioned that they didn't come earlier because they thought the practice, "only saw malignant cancer patients". Sometimes we need to be mindful of our own medically oriented biases. You need to describe your services to people who are not in the medical field in such a way that they understand what services you provide, and what services you don't.

## Place Utility

Place utility refers to providing a location where your patients can go to receive your services. Your marketing plan *strives to ensure that patients can obtain services/treatment in the most efficient and convenient way.* For one of us, a standard office has worked well; for the other, a hospital environment without a dedicated office is sufficient to offer very specialized services. Here, as part of the initial exercise we articulated in Chapter 3, your particular type of practice will dictate what location works best for you. If you wish to serve a particular segment of the population, your office may need to be in a part of town that is easily accessible to that population. In contrast, if you are a subspecialist who will attempt to garner a wide area of referrals, changing your location to better address this population will most likely be required. But remember, you must know your market segment well and limit the resources expended/planned *to what you can afford* in order to address that particular patient population.

In addition, there are many types of office settings that have arisen. In addition to the standard office with dedicated staff and services rendered by a given provider or set of providers, many models have emerged based on both technologic advancements and provider preferences. Electronic/telehealth offices now exist where patients only access providers through virtual means, and everything is done through a sophisticated electronic health record, from visits, to prescriptions, to billing. There are also models where providers utilize dedicated shared space for only physicians/providers, where examination/procedure rooms is/are rented out for a given provider for a specific time period (e.g., once per week), saving on the need to put together an entire office and yet providing both medical and minor surgical services. There are other hybrid models as well, including the return of house calls with/without paraprofessional services.

Our recommendation is first to consider what model is best for you as a provider, and don't bite off more than you can chew – create your financial model conservatively on the basis of patient numbers that will allow you to grow with time. It's better to start small and expand as your revenue increases, rather than to start big and dig a financial hole that you have to climb your way out of. Your bank account and financial statements will thank you.

## Time Utility

Time utility refers to the *availability of your services at a particular time of day (or night).* This has changed markedly over the past decade, and now accessibility is not only in person but also virtual and through electronic messaging. The wonderful thing about private practice is that you define this based on how you want to practice medicine, and where you wish to practice. As an example, one of us only practices one week a month within a hospital infrastructure with a highly specialized expertise, with the rest of the month dedicated to other medical and nonmedical pursuits. The flexibility is freeing and certainly would not be available if employed within a corporate practice.

The other of us practices four days a week in a physical office and provides a mix of in-person and telehealth services.

## Information Utility

Finally, information utility involves the *communication of information to your patients.* To be clear, your marketing plan describes a practice method that articulates what services you wish to promote; however, in addition, it also allows you to get feedback and understand if your services are addressing the unmet needs of patients who are either receiving your services or those who might be interested in your services. The huge level of emphasis on patient reviews of providers has pushed this to a new level, with some insurers using the feedback in these forums as the basis of being part of a given network. These reviews can be a helpful way to learn how you can modify your services, within reasonable limits, and something you can use to further evaluate whether it makes pragmatic and financial sense (see Chapter 5 for NPV evaluation). Of course, you also may have to deal with negative reviews, and that will be discussed in the context of customer relationship management (CRM, Chapter 9). Nonetheless, you can choose how you respond to these reviews, including whether you want to change the services you provide in your practice.

Thus, having defined your patient population (i.e., market segment) and economic utility, along with the differentiators from Chapter 3, you can now create your marketing plan as the "Marketing Mix".

## The Marketing Mix

The marketing mix is *the strategy* that brings the patients and the physicians/providers together to create a transaction. As noted in earlier chapters, the terminology used is the "Four Ps", specifically, *product, place, promotion,* and *price.* Before lamenting that this is yet more vocabulary to learn, realize that all of this is based on the previous section, so there's nothing to be afraid of here. We're now organizing this into a specific set of components that can be planned and constructed as a strategic process.

## Product

Your product is the services you want to provide to your patients. You are offering unique services that solve a problem for your patients. This is why they are coming to see you. It is paramount that you understand your patient's perception – they need to know what the service is that you will be providing, *rather than what you believe it to be.* You have to use your previous experience, whether that comes from years of practice or from residency/fellowship, to understand your patients in a granular manner and match their needs and wants to the services and characteristics of your practice. You need to articulate what services you will provide. As noted, one of us was missing a key component of their own patient population by focusing too much on what his patient population was thought to be, rather than focusing on what the perception of his patients was about the services he was providing.

Indeed, you need to structure your services to address the patient population you want to target. This is called *positioning,* which is the concept of emphasizing your services to your patients. Such positioning will derive from both the *primary* characteristics of your services (i.e., the basic service such as psychiatric medication management) *and any auxiliary services* (i.e., any additional services such as intravenous ketamine infusions or transcranial magnetic stimulation).

Note that regardless of what services you're offering, there are both *tangible* and *intangible* aspects to any offering, viz., conceptualizing positioning as *a solution for the customer is the appropriate reference point.* As a result, positioning describes a value proposition for the patient, based on a careful mixture of the primary and auxiliary characteristics of your services. So if your practice is offering pharmacologic treatments for neuropathy but also includes more advance procedural modalities, such as ultrasound, your overall positioning is as a provider who offers high-level standard of care as well as advanced treatment options, thus you offer multiple treatment options for a patient with neuropathy.

Often, the use of the term *brand* is part of positioning and strategy. The brand (or branding activity) represents an identification of a service (e.g., by name, symbol) with the physician/practitioner. It is a key item not only for identification purposes, but as a conceptual differentiator of one practice from another. Brand equity cannot be underemphasized; it is similar to reputation in the practice world, something patients *trust* will satisfy a given need. For both of us, it's what we stand for and *what we want patients to think when they think of our respective brands.*

We have seen huge brand equity in practices that are well-aware of the customers' needs, from a live person answering the phones to the excellent care that has been written up (and advertised) in numerous lay publications, driving both referrals and revenues. We have also seen losses of patients to practices who have all but abandoned CRM with lack of responsiveness to calls, endless call loops, and lack of a functioning patient portal with withering patient numbers and revenues, in a purchased practice where physicians are only employees. The important aspect of brand is to create a symbol representing the brand and functionally support it on everything related to the practice, from written correspondence to lab coats, and create excellent service associated with it. Make the symbol stand for reputation and goodwill!

## Place

We have discussed place numerous times, and for good reason; it's something you must think through carefully based on the type of practice you wish to create and how you wish to create it. As well, and more broadly, we think of place as anything that touches the service – how the services are communicated, to how the patients access the practice (e.g., by phone and/or by website). The compilation of these activities is called a "channel". These channels are used to create efficiencies in marketing by minimizing the distribution costs of the service, yet provide the target customer (e.g., patients, referring providers) with accessibility and opportunity for use or acquisition of the service. In other words, *place uses channels to communicate the services you are offering and allows patients to access those services.* To be clear, your place strategy, in addition to where/how you practice, also includes every avenue of communication related to what you offer and how your patients can obtain your services.

So, the channels you use must support your available services. All of your place efforts will target the channels used to promote your services (see the section Promotion below) and the customer service (CRM) support of your services. Knowing the channels used by patients is a key component, since that's where you will utilize much of your resources in marketing, whether that's phone services, internet scheduling, hospital personal efforts, etc. We believe this is something that can be done by you initially, using medical marketing consultants, but may be outsourced with close oversight subsequently *when you are satisfied* with how the channels are being addressed.

## Promotion

Promotion is the key tenet for the marketing strategy. Promotion is based on a detailed knowledge of the customer and marketplace and represents *the communication of your services to the patient* (how you satisfy the unmet medical need). These communications will inform, remind, and/or persuade patients about your services, using components of the "promotional mix", such as *advertising, personal selling, (sales) promotion, and public relations* (see Table 6.3). You can use many different components to create your promotions, and utilizing the most recent types of channels is key to your promotional strategy. Without putting too fine a point on this, accessing marketing consultants initially who have experience in practice message dissemination is important in this instance; while physicians/providers typically have less need than other industries to advertise, it is wise to have a promotional strategy when starting your private practice (and may be as simple as communicating to hospital generalists about your services).

Without a doubt, promotion engenders a significant dependence on *communication.*

There are four main components to this communication: the source, the message, the medium, and the receiver. In addition, two other components are important: *response* and *feedback.*

In your case, you have already designed your services and articulated them in form utility (e.g., "PracticeCo treats general psychiatric illnesses with the most cutting-edge techniques, led by a psychiatrist with 20+ years of experience, and available at a central location downtown both in-person and virtually"). This idea/concept is then converted into a *message* ("Our practice, PracticeCo, is the most advanced in the Tri-state area and treats all types of depression"), which has your service description, your positioning, your place, as well as your brand. You then summarize this through your patients' channels, encoding the idea or concept to be delivered with words and symbols ("Experience, Expertise, Results. PracticeCo: *Your* Practice"). In summary, you act as the *source* of the message, and then identify the appropriate channel (e.g., website, AARP placements, and networking at the hospital) *via* an appropriate *medium* (e.g., internet, advertisements with search engine optimization, talks to PCP doctors at the hospital) by which the maximum number of target receivers (e.g., referring physicians/patients) will receive and decode (i.e., interpret) the message being delivered. Once delivered, you can *measure* the response to a given message (e.g., appointments, both new and return visits) as well as solicit feedback (i.e., reaction to the delivered message from the source in the practice website, other forums).

## Price

Price, like the other components of the practice, has changed dramatically over the past few years. Negotiated contracts with third-party payors are one of the key forms of reimbursement for providers. It is axiomatic that negotiations should be done with the knowledge of conventional rates paid in the demographic area where you are working, but also with the understanding of the population and the rates of reimbursement prevalent in the area. Moreover, as noted previously, it is highly suggested that you negotiate contracts before starting your practice, or you will be under pressure to take the first offer from each insurer, which usually is a low-ball offer, and you won't have time to investigate the level of patient penetrance each insurer might have in your area.

In addition, the models available today vary from cash only, to "Direct Primary Care", to concierge medicine. *The "economic utility" of your services will drive what type of reimbursement you might want to accept in your practice.* For example, about one half of psychiatric practices in the United States are cash only. A growing number of primary care practices use a membership model that includes basic laboratory tests and unlimited visits, usually scheduled within 24 hours. Some concierge practices require significant upfront payments plus a membership fee for 24-hour access to a given provider. Every practice is different, and one unique aspect of private practice is you can choose how and to what degree you want to practice in each of the myriad choices of reimbursement that are available. Some of the factors you may want to consider are those mentioned earlier in this chapter (see Tables 6.1 and 6.2) as well as what levels of services you will be providing (see Table 6.4). The level of flexibility is high, and based on the research you've already done, it's a matter of what your personal preference is vis-a-vis expectations of what your costs are anticipated to be. Remember: you want to generate a profit!

With the efforts from Chapters 3 and 4, and what you've done here, you now have the components of your marketing plan that you can either put in place, if you have the background, or seek assistance from those experienced in channels that you and your consultants anticipate your patients will access in order to seek out your services.

If you've gotten this far, you might realize that what you have just completed has previously been done for you in your most recent work experience! What becomes clear is that you can be as busy as you want to be, and you can create your own position in your own place.

**Table 6.3 Components of the Promotional Mix**

| |
|---|
| **Advertising:** Any paid form of persuasive message in a nonpersonal medium where the service is identified (e.g., website with search engine optimization) |
| **Personal Selling:** An in-person presentation meant to inform and persuade others to influence a transaction (e.g., referrals) |
| **Sales Promotion:** Activities (other than personal selling) that provide incentives to effect a use of the service (e.g., free cholesterol screening) |
| **Public Relations:** Usually unpaid presentations and stimulation of activities to managing informing of the service to a media (e.g., talk to local community leaders about depression) |

**Table 6.4 Examples of Pricing Strategies**

| |
|---|
| *Cash Pricing* |
| The same services can be charged different prices for if paying by cash vs. third-party payers. |
| *Competitive Pricing* |
| Pricing decisions can be made based on what competitors are charging. Such decisions may involve matching, discounting, or premium pricing based on product positioning (e.g., 10% below neighboring providers for ECT). |
| *Product-Line Pricing* |
| Using a multitude of services, maximize the profitability of the entire line of services rather than the component parts (e.g., "loss leader" pricing, bundling multiple services and charging less than the combined price). |
| *Psychological Pricing* |
| This method of pricing is based on the patient's perception of certain components of the services that are tied to the price. These perceptions can be related to the developed brand/reputation. Examples include: "prestige effect" (higher quality associated with higher price), "isolation effect" (placement of moderate priced items next to higher priced items), and odd pricing" (the use of odd numbers, such as \$2.99 vs. \$3.00, to give the perception of a less expensive product). |

The beauty of private practice is you get to decide how and what you want to practice, without being pushed to do things you don't want to do. Again, as you design your marketing plan, you're addressing what you think you do best, with an understanding of the size of the patient population you're addressing. Assuming they match, this is a much better scenario than being in a corporate setting where you are forced to be all things to all taskmasters who have no domain expertise!

## Checklist

From Chapters 3 and 4:

What problem are you solving?
What is the overall way you'll solve the problem?
What market will you target?
Who is the competition? Who ISN'T the competition? How are you unique? What's your competitive advantage?
Why will patients opt to pick your practice?

*Complete the remaining business plan questions from template*

From this chapter:
**Market segmentation**: *Who, why*

Unmet medical need
What market will you target (from above)
Size of market
Ability to access the market
Ability to measure market size and success of marketing effort (new patients)
Identify demographics, income levels, types of insurance, lifestyle, usage patterns anticipated, other required care (primary vs. specialty)

**Form utility**: *The offering and anticipated perception*

What are you offering, and what do you think your patients believe your offering to be (what problem are you solving, and how from above).
Have you checked with nonmedical personnel about your services?

**Place utility:** *The location of services vis-a-vis the target market*

For the type of practice you wish to have, is the place of service appropriate? Will your resources be sufficient in marketing to reach your desired patients?
What kind of place are you interested in pursuing? Consider the patients you are targeting and the demographic involved.

**Time utility**: *Addressing availability for services*

What is the availability for your services? How will that match your patients' needs?

**Information utility**: *The type of information you want to provide to your patients*

What kind of information can you communicate to your patients? What emphasis do you want to make in the information you communicate? How will you do this?

**Marketing mix**: *The strategic plan*

**Product**: *The patient's perception of the solution to their problem*
The perceived solution by the patient being provided by the physician/provider to the patient; the positioning, that is, of the primary and auxiliary services of the practice; the value to the patient
The (developing) brand that differentiates your practice from others; what you stand for

**Place**: *The location of the services and influences of different channels*
Broadly, how any aspects of the service are accessed and communicated toward bringing a patient into the practice; it encompasses not only the patient's perception and experience but how information is accessed and how patients are sent to the practice (e.g., referrals) viz., channels to the practice.

**Promotion**: *Any activity communicating your services*
The use of advertising, personal selling, sales promotion, and public relations to communicate your services and their value to your patients
Taking form utility and creating a message encompassing your positioning and brand, through the channels your patients use to gather information

**Price**: *The anticipated reimbursement plan based on articulated models*
Determination of the mechanism of reimbursement, from third-party payers to concierge medicine, depending on your preferred model, matched with the type of medicine and profitability

# Chapter 7

# Negotiation

## Introduction

Some look on negotiation as an opportunity, one where there is a potential to articulate what one wants; others look upon it with horror, filled with conflict and argument without resolution. Still others think it is of limited or no value, since when dealing with large, bureaucratic institutions, there isn't any way to negotiate. One of the things we have heard the most in our travels and discussions with other physicians is that, "there's no way to negotiate", or, "you can't negotiate – it's take it or leave it". Well, in fact, after years of working in health care, and doing deals from employment contracts to federal legislation, we can assure you that there *is* the ability to negotiate. In fact, in any situation where there are diverse interests, one never gets what one needs, or what one thinks one deserves; one gets only what one negotiates.

## Operating Definitions

So what is negotiation? There are a number of definitions, but making the large assumption that both parties *want* to come to an agreement, we can define it as a *process*; this process is one where there is an exchange of ideas in order to obtain an agreement that has mutual benefit. Looking at the process of negotiation allows us to better understand the dynamics that result in a negotiated agreement, and how good negotiators come to agreement with other parties, no matter how diverse the interests.

So, to understand the process, we need to understand some vocabulary (see Glossary at the end of the chapter). These are descriptive aspects helping show how and why things go well or awry during the process. Most simply, when two parties come together to discuss a potential agreement, each has a particular point of view, and the best thing to do in any negotiation is *to define it clearly to oneself before the outset, that is, know what you want before negotiating!* So, for example, if we're

DOI: 10.4324/9781003685623-7

talking about buying and selling an item, both parties will have a *resistance point or reservation price* (RP); if you're the buyer, you won't go any higher, and if the seller, you won't go any lower. This is the "bottom line" that each party has, from which one otherwise "walks away" from a deal.

Now there is a space between the RP's of the buyer and seller, obviously. This is called the zone of potential agreement (ZOPA). If the buyer is willing to pay $100 or less for an item, and the seller is willing to sell for $98 and more, the ZOPA is between $98 and $100. Of course, this is positive; however, the ZOPA can be negative as well. If the ZOPA is positive, then doing a deal is better than walking away; if the ZOPA is negative, walking away is better than doing the deal. The most important aspect of this description is that the first thing in any negotiation is *to know your RP, and if possible, try to understand the RP of the other party.*

An aside on this is the danger for new negotiators, viz., *agreement bias*. Here, for reasons of inexperience, fatigue, perspective, etc., an agreement is made *despite* a negative ZOPA. The *perception* often is that because we (the parties) are *supposed* to come to an agreement, since we've spent a lot of effort and time discussing it, we consciously or unconsciously adjust our RP despite no new information. Because of this we need to be very clear about what our RP is and how best to articulate it.

## How Do We Define Our RP?

Shaping our RP thus is the next most important aspect in any preparation to negotiate. We determine our RP by defining the *best alternative to a negotiated agreement* (BATNA). The first and foremost rule of negotiations is that you must assess your BATNA and what you will do if it's determined you want to walk away. The RP is the *quantification* of your BATNA, and your BATNA is the stake in the ground with your alternative ("plan B") executed if no agreement takes place. Simply put, accept deals where the conditions are better than your BATNA and reject ones that are less than your BATNA. The key here is that your BATNA is not aspirational; it's absolutely *objective*, which will allow you to point out the facts during negotiation. Note, however, that your BATNA can change, based on new data or facts; however, it should NOT change based on techniques to sway your emotions or devalue your perspective. Thus, you can see how your BATNA is the basis of your negotiation and how important it is in order to define your position. That's why it is worth the effort to spend time BEFORE GETTING TO THE NEGOTIATION TABLE to clearly verbalize your BATNA; you must articulate your BATNA *and* what outcomes would be *better*. It's important to understand that this may require doing quantification of nonobjective aspects into objective aspects (like ancillary benefits of a purchase, for example).

So once you know the RP and BATNA, you have begun the journey toward negotiation. Some key aspects are as follows:

1 *Revealing your BATNA to the other side*: In general, one doesn't reveal one's BATNA since overall it's unlikely that the other party will offer you more than your RP. It's best to only consider revealing IF your alternative to a negotiated deal is very, very good, and you want to see if a deal can be done that will match or exceed it. That's obviously a very strong position to be in. As well, the other side of the coin is also reasonable to reveal your BATNA – if no deal looks imminent, and you're about to walk out and conclude negotiations, you can *consider* revealing your BATNA, IF you feel the other party is sincere. But you have to be ready to walk away in any event.

2 *Create an aspiration point (AP)*: This is the value you aspire to achieve within the negotiation. However, it must be realistic and possible, not a pie-in-the-sky idea. Here again, it's about

data and facts (you're seeing a theme here). You need to know whatever market conditions prevail as well as anticipate the other side's BATNA. For now, just beware that if you over-aspire because of emotion or some other nonobjective means, you can lose credibility in the negotiation. On the other hand, under-aspiring can lead to getting something less than you want but then regretting it (and not being able to go back to the table!). Finally, one has to be careful of the psychological tendency to want what the other side doesn't want to give and instead devalue what they do want to give – *aka* reactive devaluation. That's why you want to be clear in your own mind what's your AP, and as importantly, what it isn't.

3 *The anchoring effect, or "Should we make the first offer?"*: There is significant discussion about this in negotiation circles, but the idea is that there is cognitive bias in negotiations where the *initial* offer can "set the anchor" in the context of the negotiation. Again, understanding the rationale and market is important in this regard, although certainly it may be more aligned with perception than objective facts. Hence, always come to a negotiation with a first offer and be ready to offer it to set that anchor. If the other party beats you to it, rather than fall into the negotiation around their anchor, reanchor the discussion with your planned first offer.
4 *Beware of the "winner's curse"*: This concept is one where you set your RP and AP so low that you anchor yourself so that you "win" a very low value position. This is especially something prone to those who are conflict averse and would prefer to allow themselves to come to an agreement with suboptimal terms than continue to negotiate with a firm understanding of their RP and AP. As an extension, set your RP and BATNA, but don't let your RP = AP! Finally, one has to be careful of being anchored by one's own BATNA – that's why you determined your first offer initially!

## The Pie Isn't Just About Dividing It Up

In general, when we negotiate, what we're trying to do is find the way we can *expand the pie* rather than just distribute the pie. The key is to determine whether

1 There is only a *distributive* issue present, that is, a zero-sum game;
2 A *compatible* (but *non*-competitive similarities and not mutually exclusive), where can *expand* the pie (both parties *want the same thing*); or
3 Where there is a potential for *integrative* aspects, where the pie can *expand* and *both* parties can gain.

The bedrock of negotiation is to find for each issue on the table whether it is distributive, compatible, or integrative in nature. Further, the point is to figure out for each issue which is the priority. One key definition here is *competitive* negotiation; that's when a party is actively only looking out for the interests of their own side and trying to grab everything they can as a "competition" rather than an integrative approach. Recognizing this is important in order to call it out and create integrative solutions instead (see X-card below).

Obviously, the key is to create integration since that increases the size of the pie, and one does this by prioritizing the issues, understanding the other side's priorities (and hence their BATNA), expanding the issues, and then trading to create the most value *collectively*.

As a result, one has to get all the issues out on the table at the outset and not identify them piecemeal or both parties will end up with only distributive options. The key here is to understand all issues that are important for each side, *rather than* just the points within each individual issue, something that some less experienced negotiators try to address rather than the bigger prioritization picture. And let's get something out of the way – all of this should be done without judgment of relative prioritization – by either party. Denigrating the other side's priorities is not fruitful for anyone trying to get a deal done – only by acknowledging the other side's priorities can your side figure out if you can create that integrative solution. Hence, logic, conceptive frameworks, and what you consider operational judgments have no role here. Only making sure you've expanded the issues, prioritized your issues, understood the other side's priorities, and then being able to trade are the key activities.

And this is how we get to understand, at least conceptually, the other side's BATNA. If the incremental revelation of interests by overall discussion can create context, then we can see which issues are most relevant to the other party and note that in our own perspective. We can compare them to our own BATNA and determine which issues are distributive, competitive, and potentially integrative. Certainly, and importantly, we can and should also do this *a priori*, in order to be prepared for the negotiation, and change our perspectives as we get more information. As has been stated many times herein, being prepared for the negotiation is key. We include a modification of a preparatory handout in the Appendix so you can be ready for a given negotiation based on the questions asked.

A word about sharing your priorities. It's best to acknowledge that *all* issues are relevant to your side, but issues X, Y, and Z are *more important* such that you don't fall into the trap of having issues dismissed. Of course, it depends on the issues – and whether they are distributive/compatible in nature, which prevents you from revealing certain information since it's either a zero sum or the same interests are desired. While integrative approaches are important for cooperation, they leave you open for competitive exploitation. Studies have shown, however, that in order to get to the best outcomes, both sides cooperating in an integrative fashion do the best; competing against each other leads to constriction of outcomes since you limit the number of issues you can get on the table, that is, trade.

Hence, the guidance from years of research is to approach negotiation by playing your "Y-card" first, that is, make your opening salvo one of cooperation and attempts at integration. Your next move will mirror the approach the other party takes. If they play their "X-card", that is, they are competitive rather than cooperative, you play your X-card to show you are "provocable". If they continue, you continue playing your X-card. However, if they play their Y-card initially, you continue with that perspective. Similarly, if they back down and play their Y-card after they've played their X-card, you reciprocate to show you value cooperation rather than competition. What you are basically doing is influencing the negotiation to show that by cooperating, the discussions move toward agreement rather than escalating toward only competing or distributive outcomes. Always create that cooperative tone as early in the negotiation as soon as possible; this may require a pre-meeting to agree on what the process is to use in discussion. Regardless, setting the tone for cooperation is important when starting a negotiation, and something well worth some initial discussion before outlining the issues.

## Tactics

Often times we've heard that, well, all of this is fine, but how do we start a discussion once we've come to the table? Clearly, a lot of this is about preparation. One has to have done one's homework about the objective aspects of RP, AP, BATNA, and what we expect the other side to want in turn. In the Appendix of this chapter, we outline the key aspects one should think about *before* going into a negotiation, adapted from the MIT Sloan School of Management-Harvard Business School Seven

Elements of Negotiation. The preparation should always be done well before one goes into the negotiation, in order to prepare you for what you will ask for, what you think the other side will ask for, what issues you think will be brought up, how you think the other side will respond, and how you will respond to what they might bring up. This is a template easy to use, and various forms have been modified and utilized in many negotiations in the past. Always be prepared when going into the negotiation with such a template so you avoid shortchanging yourself on your RP/AP.

When entering into the negotiation, always start with discussing the *interests of the parties*, rather than positions *per se* – you are trying to get the cooperation rubric clear as the operational process. Making the other side understand you're trying to give them what they want is clear but letting them know that you can't do that unless you know what it is has to be the message. This is a marathon, not a sprint, so ensuring your own *incremental revelation* of your own information is *reciprocated* allows for a cycle of cooperation. It's usually recommended NOT to try to hit the hardest issues first but rather address the easier ones so (hopefully!) both parties can show their ability to come to *tentative* agreements (always – further trading may be necessary). Again, get all those issues out before starting to discuss individual ones.

Finally, while a cooperative tone is what one is hoping for, always verify to ensure the key information is flowing both ways in the discussion. This is to ensure that cooperation is going on both ways. Clarify what you think is being communicated to you in order to avoid any misunderstandings during the cooperation process.

## Curve Balls and Deceptive Negotiation

To date, you've created your RP, AP, and BATNA; learned anchoring and the challenges within it; as well as developed an understanding of how cooperation is the better way to negotiate; but you've also come to understand when to play your X-card and when to play your Y-card. These are important components to your burgeoning skills as a negotiator and will serve you well in many different situations.

Of course, not everyone negotiates the same way, and some have less candor and ethics than others. Some negotiators are taught that using tactics that will throw you off your cooperative nature is the way to get the "best" deal for their side – we've seen everything from not telling parties about changes made in written agreements to frankly lying about "that's the final offer". We have to see this as a challenge but also as what it is – *unsavory techniques to get you to agree.* Let's talk about approaches in dealing with some more common examples of difficult tactics.

### *Intimidation and Anger (Potentially Most Damaging to a Negotiation)*

Anger can be either real or feigned (tactical). The key is not to get caught up in it and escalating it to create an impasse; at the same time, you do NOT want to give into it and change your RP/AP. In this case, you must see if integrative approaches can still be used, but not before you assess whether this is something the other side is doing for effect purposes. If you feel the anger is feigned, match it with your own capability to be angry, but realigning the discussion toward integrative solutions. Noting, "our efforts can be to find a solution, or we can continue to yell at each other" shows our ability to continue to be integrative despite the tactic being used by the other side.

There are instances where the other side is *truly* angry. We see this in situations where the anger gradually increases due to frustration, and the other side perceives you are not acknowledging their position nor responding to their communication. In short, they feel they're being ignored. One really has to ensure that in this case there is empathetic listening on your side, rather than responding in anger like you would with tactical anger. Determining true vs. tactical anger is clearly important to ensure continuing an integrative approach. You might guess wrong, but coming back to an integrative approach is the important point.

Examples of anger that is feigned usually are associated with one issue that generates an emotional response – it comes as a surprise. With non-feigned anger, one typically sees frustration building on the other side, with comments of "you're not listening to me" or "you don't understand". Hearing such comments really should alert you toward slowing down and ensuring you can repeat and articulate the counter party position so you truly understand and can communicate such to them.

## Extreme Position (Most Common)

Suffice to say, being prepared is a key aspect to any negotiation. Those who don't know history are doomed to relive it; same thing about negotiations. If you don't know what a fair offer in the discussion is, the tactic being used is to try to have you reconsider your BATNA/RP as well as AP. That's why defining this up front with data is key, so that you have the credibility when you counter their proposal. Most often you have to have this as the *second* thing you discuss; you don't throw it out there at the beginning but instead call out the tactic and play your X-card about insisting on realistic terms prior to attempting an integrative approach. Countering such an offer forces the other party to continue on Y-card terms rather than trying to downgrade their position with reason.

An example of the extreme position is the purchase of an automobile; the salesperson will suggest a price or will note how another price is so low that no competitor can match it. If you've done your initial work, you'll know what prices are reasonable and those which aren't, and you can call this out right away without noting your databases that have the price for the dealership and costs of options.

## Snow Job

This is the opposite of the extreme offer, where instead of presenting an offer that is far off the mark, the attempt is to overwhelm you with "data" that ostensibly justifies their position. The fact is that it is meant to try to weaken your position of credibility by having a significant volume of information rather than either credible or relevant aspects. Again, doing one's homework is key, and knowing your own credible position is very important once again. As you can see, being prepared before getting to the table with tangible evidence for your position is paramount.

If you are unaware or unclear on certain aspects of the information presented, you must ask questions about the relevance of the material thrown at you and determine what is fluff and what isn't. Never make commitments based on information you don't understand. You can take these aspects under advisement and can be prepared to address the details after you've conferred with your own experts. Most of us who have some level of technical training are good at finding inconsistencies, and this is one where you really want to listen carefully to identify such.

An example of such a tactic is negotiating price of equipment. You may hear numerous technical descriptions of the specific device, many of which aren't even something you're familiar with. Asking questions, clarifying the importance of these aspects, and ensuring you understand the nature of these "qualities" and their relative importance are, again, the preparation that you will have done prior to entering into the negotiation, with always the ability to get more advice before commitments.

## *The Bogey*

This is essentially a misdirection tactic, where the other side takes a specific issue and negotiates very hard on it, claiming high levels of importance to the deal. In fact, it's unimportant, and they use it for a bargaining chip and agree to concede for another trade. While it may be difficult to initially recognize, you can detect it in retrospect when there is a sudden change where after such an intense discussion on the issue, another issue is brought up and they're willing to "sacrifice" the bogey issue. The expectation, of course, is that you will in turn give something of relevance up as well. Once again, being prepared with your own BATNA/RP/AP and anticipating theirs is key; ask questions on the importance of the issue to the other side, or what caused the introduction of the new issue in the first place. This is also the reason at the outset you want to discuss all the issues and not each issue *seriatim* (i.e., in sequential order). If you find that there is limited information that can be shared, particularly about why a so vociferously negotiated point is willing to be sacrificed, you've probably encountered a bogey. Treat the issue appropriately.

A classic bogey is in employment negotiations, where employers use this tactic to divert initial attention from an important issue (e.g., salary) by playing up an alternative issue (e.g., vacation time). They then "concede" on giving "more" vacation in exchange for less salary or other compensation. Knowing the market for these items is an important counter for these tactics, and of course, questioning what is really important to the other side.

## *Good Cop/Bad Cop*

Here, it's either two parties or two perspectives that are worked on as a team approach, where one offers conciliatory position(s) and the other offers much less and is hostile and threatening. Usually, the hostile aspect comes first, then the more reasonable one. It's a situation where the "good cop" is trying to gain the other side's trust to win a concession, since otherwise you're stuck negotiating with the "bad cop". Psychologically, this is effective since we tend to want to negotiate and agree with those we like and are like us or friendly to us – the good – and are averse to those who are unpleasant – the bad. Moreover, the offering from the good cop seems more reasonable on a relative basis compared to that of the bad cop.

Dealing with this tactic is to call it out. You need to specifically identify the two perspectives in the negotiation (rather than good cop/bad cop) and note that you would like to be more integrative in the discussion. This allows for recognition by the other side of your familiarity of various tactics and your emphasis of creating value within the negotiation as an integrative approach.

Good cop/bad cop negotiations occur in many situations. Again, in employment agreement negotiations there can be one person who grills you and tries to put you in a defensive situation, where the other negotiator says little but offers you coffee during the negotiation, and then asks you to consider a concession outside of the actual negotiation. You have to be ready to see this and counter it with the appropriate comments on an integrative solution.

## *Take It or Leave It*

The use of this tactic is essentially telling you the other party isn't particularly interested in negotiating, and/or is running out of resources (e.g., time), or wants to effect a power play in the discussion. In fact, most negotiations are not that cut and dry, and most often are manifest because of impatience or just a hard bargaining tactic by the counterparty. There are several steps to deal with such a tactic, depending on who has the most investment in the relationship. In any event, first and foremost if you consider this an important relationship/deal, continuing to negotiate is the most effective way to create an integrative solution. To do this, it's best to ask broad questions, like the consequences, if there is no agreement. Also, asking an open-ended question to assess the degree to which the counterparty is committed to walking away in a nonthreatening way, usually with credible examples, is something that can be done to continue the negotiation. Finding ways to offer a counter that is value adding is the goal. Nonetheless, if your BATNA is well-defined, and you know you are at a point where either (1) the offer on the table exceeds your BATNA or (2) the offer is less than your BATNA, you can choose to accept or decline as appropriate and end the negotiation. If you choose the latter, it is important to decide, if the other party is then willing to come back to the table, whether you would prefer to deal with such a negotiator who is willing to put their own reputation on the line to try to force you to agree to a hard line.

We see this often in situations where there is a larger party negotiating with an individual (including personal experience). Defining your BATNA and doing your preparation work is clearly to your advantage here and knowing how far you are from a ZOPA helps give you perspective on how likely a negotiation is going to succeed. One of us has walked away from an employment negotiation since "contracts at XX institution are non-negotiable" only to have them try to return to the table after we'd moved on.

There are other tactics as well, from aggressive belittling of your position, to threats, to lying. Again, by being prepared for the negotiation, with a fact-based, objective BATNA, and the tactic for clarification and integrative solutions, you can best negotiate for your own and the other party's benefit. Being able to identify and if necessary call out a negotiation tactic is important so your own position isn't manipulated by others. Knowledge is power in these cases.

## The Tactic of Lying

One of the questions that comes up, usually at the end of a discussion about negotiation, is the issue of lying. In the MIT-Harvard Course on Negotiation, it's presented that essentially you *can* take the perspective that everyone is lying in a negotiation; that's just part of the game. But, importantly, the other two perspectives are that some will only stick with the truth even if it costs their side by doing so, and still others note that "it depends" and being an absolutist is unwise. Further, if the other side is in a "compete" mode for the best aspects for themselves only, this can cause escalation on both sides toward extreme measures; further, if there is no potential relationship in the future, this can be a rationale to be deceptive.

In general, one has to determine this individually, but certainly considerations about effects on self-image, generalizability of such a tactic, and effects on how others might perceive deceptive actions certainly are considerations worthwhile in your approach. While we certainly *consider* these approaches during a negotiation and may even unconsciously move from one approach to another, we must be cognizant of our own ethical boundaries, from damaging or even destroying our reputation and the relationship with the counterparty to the point of being liable for fraud in the extreme of circumstances. In any negotiation, being very observant of one's own behavior is important in the attempt to find a value-added integrative solution for all parties involved.

## Appendix: Preparation Points for Negotiation

For *both* our side and the counterparty, answer the following questions with as much detail as possible; for the counterparty, if answers are unknown, try to make some assumptions and come up with anticipated answers.

1 Who are the stakeholders and their underlying interests? What is the best approximation of the priorities? What are the compatible interests? What are the differences, both objective and subjective?
2 What are the BATNAs/RP/AP? What are the alternatives to negotiation? Can the BATNA be better served away from negotiating? What are the ways one can confirm or reject our impressions of the other side's positions?
3 What is the best way to discuss the overall deal components rather than each individual component? Are there frameworks we can consider that are possible to come to for integrative agreements? Can we exploit our key differences?
4 What are the objective criteria the parties can point to and are most credible? What are the standards each side will try to use? How will we be able to steer toward our standards/objective measures? Are there questions not well-researched currently or without standards that we should put aside for now?
5 What are the commitments you can allow yourself to make, and what will you NOT make? What do you anticipate are the commitments that can be made on the other side? Are the people we are meeting with decision-makers – if not, who are the decision-makers and why aren't we meeting with them?
6 Is this relationship a one-off, or is it with a future? Is this relationship ideal for the topic/s of negotiation? Should the parties use intermediaries?
7 Can we create an environment of brainstorming without judgment? Can we encourage ideas to allow for potential integrative solutions? Are the modes of communication allowing us to be creative? Are we both trying to reiterate in order for both sides to feel understood and perspectives respected? Are there perceptions each side holds that need to be discussed, which are either objective or subjective, that get in the way of brainstorming?

## Glossary

**Anchor/Anchoring**
An opening position, from which a negotiator may move away (positively or negatively) during a negotiation. The choice of an anchor may be based on inaccurate information, be tactically determined, and/or meant to mislead.

**Aspiration Point (AP)**
An optimal point that a party hopes to achieve. It is often the most favorable result and more than the minimum acceptable outcome.

**Best Alternative to a Negotiated Agreement (BATNA)**
BATNA is your walk-away position and the most ideal course of action when the negotiation fails.

**Bottom Line**
This refers to the minimum or maximum point each party will accept before they fully walk away from negotiations.

**Competitive Negotiation**
A technique of negotiation that tends to have little concern for the other party and has as it's primary objective "winning" as much as possible with most if not all positions considered distributive.

**Distributive Negotiation**
A negotiation technique and/or type that seeks to gain at the opponent's loss; a zero-sum game. Any situation in which one person's gain is exactly equal to the opponent's loss is considered distributive. Haggling over $1 is an example of distributive negotiation.

**Haggling Strategy**
Haggling is an approach to bargaining relentlessly for the purpose of getting more or giving less without concern for the relationship.

**Integrative Negotiation**
The integrative negotiation is a type of collaborative negotiation style characterized by the intent of identifying positions and prioritization resulting in a win-win for both parties.

**Reach a Consensus**
This refers to when both parties agree on a given point previously disagreed upon.

**Reservation Point/Resistance Point (RP)**
For sellers, the reservation price or value is the minimum amount they are prepared to accept; for buyers, it's the value they are willing to spend. In other words, it is the point beyond which a party will not go.

**Ultimatum ("Take It or Leave It")**
A position articulated by one party on a position, or otherwise no agreement, in an attempt to force the other party into making a decision to either accept or walk away.

**Walk-Out/Walk-Away**
This is a situation where a party leaves the negotiating table and refuses to return. It is a deliberate tactic to compel pressure on the other party and shift the power dynamics to the one who walks out.

**Winner's Curse**
This occurs when your AP and/or RP and thus your BATNA is too low, and you accept a deal – you "win", but you could have gotten a better deal had you been more persistent or had a different anchor.

**Zone of Potential Agreement (ZOPA)**
The ZOPA is the range of reservation values and their overlap between each party in a negotiation. Marginally, it is the overlap area in which a party is willing to pay, and a party is willing to sell (positive) or the deficit between parties (negative).

# Chapter 8

# Financing a Practice

## Introduction

You've now gotten through your business plan, your marketing plan, what your budget looks like, the type of practice you wish to set up, and you've considered how to set up your payer contracts as well as scheduling *before* you start your practice – that's GREAT! This is the point where you want to consider making those plans into a reality, ***your*** reality of being in private practice. Here's where you want to consider the mechanism by which you'll raise capital for your dream. It's NOT as daunting as it sounds, since as a provider you're considered a "good" risk to lend money, since doctors typically don't go out of business (it's the same reason why real estate brokers like you too, by the way). So let's talk briefly about financing a practice through the major mechanisms used both in the past and today.

## Preparation

Parts of our initial chapters have guided you through the exercise of creating your business plan and budgets (start-up and operating). The key things to note when you're thinking about how to approach sources of capital are the following:

1. The full cost of start-up activities
2. The ongoing yearly cost to operate your practice
3. The number of months it will take to break even (costs = revenues)
4. The number of months it will take to generate a profit
5. The "cushion" needed for "just in case" issues (usually three months of revenues)

DOI: 10.4324/9781003685623-8

Now, your need for financing a practice will depend on whether you are just completing a training program, or if you've been out for a while in a practice setting. Regardless, preparation is the key.

*To reiterate*: Plan, plan, and plan some more. Negotiate your payer contracts first; put in a scheduling function after your practice has been announced (through the local hospital, medical society, AARP, etc.); hire/build small first to be ready when the clinic/OR/ambulatory center/procedure unit is ready (and so are you!).

If you're already in practice, you still need to do all the planning, as noted, but it's a bit modified. First, make sure your previous employment contract does not contain a noncompete clause (try not to have one!); you should have already prepared to have any payor contracts in your name (not the practice you work for) so you can move them to a new location. If you're hamstrung on these points, look to those activities just articulated before opening any doors, either for financing or your practice itself.

A word about *joining a group first:* There are definitely some advantages to joining a group, especially if you've read this book – have the payor contracts in your name, avoid noncompetes (certain states bar physician noncompetes, and in certain instances the Federal Trade Commission prevents them, but you'll need to check given your specific situation), and learn processes outside of patient care (e.g. scheduling, billing, collections). However, if you've already put in place a business plan and operating budget, know what kind of practice you want to set up (see below), and are prepped with scheduling and payor contracts, you've done your homework regardless of whether you are or part of a group or not, and you are ready to talk to financiers.

A last piece of advice *before* raising capital: Don't go in blind with grand aspirations. Start small, especially if you don't have a full clinic yet, have only negotiated one or two contracts from payors, or you have a noncompete that's prohibiting you from seeing the most lucrative patients. It CAN BE DONE – you may just need to use models like shared space, limit expenditures to ONLY required ones (e.g., credentialing, malpractice insurance, and licensing) until you get some revenue momentum (and even here, you must know your budgets, especially when you start to make a profit). Note that you should still make every effort to have payor contracts and scheduling in place. The latter may even be done as part of a rental agreement with the shared space – something that should be explored, but always try to have something available on the web so patients can access a schedule that fits their own. Some direct primary care practices charge monthly payments for a given set of primary care services – all of which are provided online, and this system works VERY well for them.

This discussion is to prepare you to meet with those who have money to invest and to answer the initial questions they may have. This discussion is also intended to help you with other components of your business plan that may be addressed during a meeting with financiers. So what are the sources of potential capital for your new practice?

## Banks

One of the fantastic things about being a physician is that banks love you. While starting an auto repair service, selling artisan jewelry, or opening a bakery are all wonderful businesses, they are fraught with much higher risk than seeing, evaluating, and treating patients. Those years of medical school, residency, and fellowship made a difference! Your services are needed, and that's becoming more and more acute every day.

### Programs

Most commercial banks have specific professional/physician lending programs that are much more competitive than the standard loans available to other businesses. If you are not presented with these right away, just ask. You're a low-risk customer, so many good banks will compete for your business. Clearly, though, you must look through the terms of any loan, as you would if you were taking out a personal mortgage or a home equity loan/line of credit. Issues like interest rates, prepayment penalties, personal service, and other covenants should all be scrutinized. As noted many times, READ. YOUR. CONTRACT. If you don't understand it, get clarification; if it's still not clear, get advice from someone who can help you understand it.

There are a variety of different programs, from lump sum payments to revolving lines of credit, to a hybrid between the two. Other packages we've seen are sums ("tranches") that come in regularly on a negotiated time frame (e.g., quarterly). The financing typically is structured the way you want it to be in order to address the needs of your practice. You know from your budgets *where* the money is needed most as well as *when*; use the budget you've created as your guide to determine how you want the financing to come into your practice. It goes without saying that you want the debt paid off as quickly as possible; when *starting* a practice, you should have the initial goal to be debt free and only go into debt again for positive return activities (see NPV in Chapter 5).

#### *Banker Targets*

The banks and loan officers are targeting the most competent businessperson who has created a budget, has an operating plan (business plan), with appropriate resources (e.g., place of business, marketing plan, and required personnel), and is without high levels of outstanding personnel or other debt. In other words, they want someone with a good credit score! The components used to build your business plan – patient demographics, payer mix, competitive advantage in the marketplace, and the like – are what lenders want to see, as would you if you were loaning money to someone who's starting a new business. All of this is so the lender can be quite clear that you can pay the loan back, with a reasonable amount of certainty.

### *Investors*

Another source of capital are investors. When we speak of investors, whether they be private equity firms, hospitals, other practices, or other service providers (e.g., telemedicine or internet firms), we're talking about those who are giving you money for a reason other than just capital payback with interest; it's because they want equity (part ownership of the practice), service (serve a given part of the population for whom they have an interest), extension (increased reach or diversity of services provided), or all of the above. Each of these types of investors can provide you start-up, operational, and even buy-out capital for your fledgling practice.

## What Do Investors Want?

At the core, investors all want *something* from you. This may include ownership for a percentage of the profits you make in the practice; we can talk endlessly about the type of activity that will go into this, from negotiating what the practice is worth, and how much their investment is worth, to how much they're getting at the end of the day. There may be a desire to have operational control to maximize revenues through productivity and cost savings. Access to the practice for another group's own patients (hospital, other practices) in order to serve a given population or for marketing purposes is also a key reason for investing in your practice. An extension of the latter is branding rights for your practice along with prioritization of that practice's own patients. An additional requirement for investment could be access and set up for telehealth services, including appropriate licensing, equipment, and billing infrastructure. All of the above may be obligatory, depending on the circumstances.

Your willingness to participate in such investor requirements is a function of how you want to set up your practice. These are all viable options as long as you go into it with eyes wide open. These options can be in addition to any debt you take on from a bank. And certainly, this can all be temporary as you start the new practice, with appropriate contract language of protection for you and the practice, so that you can walk away from any of this with the appropriate payback or terms that you feel are within reason. Because this is private practice, it's really up to you to decide what you want for your practice and what you're willing to do to start it, including these activities. Once again, negotiate, and READ. YOUR. CONTRACT. Understand it, be comfortable with the terms and/or find someone who can explain it all to you to your satisfaction and be sure there is an escape clause you are satisfied with.

## Ongoing Practices Require Capital as Well

Recall from Chapter 5 that you can calculate something that the practice might be willing to do in order to add value. That was the NPV (net present value), which is easily obtainable from any spreadsheet as long as you have the cost of capital percentage, the amount you have to invest into the project, and the expected revenues from the project. Whether it's new equipment, renovations, a new EHR, etc., you can figure out whether this is worth it, and whether taking on debt will be reasonable for creating more value for the practice.

Not surprisingly, the aforementioned options are the same (and more!) to garner capital for these projects. But if you are a successful practice (i.e., are profitable), you are even a *better* risk! So you have even *more* options. You can do a longer term financing deal with a bank for a lower interest rate with an amortization schedule to your advantage. You can create a deal where a hospital puts equipment in your office for you to use as compensation for seeing their patients. You can accept a machine from a company to use for your patients in order to show how valuable it is to the practice. You can agree to do a marketing clinical trial from a pharmaceutical company. The list goes on and on, and certainly if you're a successful practice these will be options for the future.

Just use the tools in Chapter 5 to ensure it is value creating and you capture any hidden costs (e.g., training time, space in the clinic, meeting with sponsors, and number of patients expected) that you may have to accommodate. And make sure your accountant also keeps you updated with regular feedback on the depreciation of your assets, since that will give you a ballpark understanding of the timing of the wear and tear on items that need periodic replacement and thus future expenditures. After all, you have to invest in your practice, so the practice captures value, and patients continue to get the best care ("mutual value creation"). Finally, you want to capture those profits into your "retained earnings" in order to minimize the amount of capital you need to access from others. Debt of one kind or another always carries a hangover on earnings – it just has to be worthwhile!

# Chapter 9

# The Art of Customer Relationship Management

## Patients Are Customers (But Don't Call Them That)

You didn't spend years studying medicine, slogging through residency, and perfecting your bedside manner just to think of your patients as "customers". That feels too corporate, too impersonal. But here's the thing – when you open a (solo) private practice, your patients are also your customers. And like any successful business, your practice thrives on customer relationship management (CRM).

The good news? Unlike big hospital systems with impersonal call centers and automated messages, you can build real relationships with your patients. The kind that keeps them coming back – and telling their friends about how you actually listen (a rare and magical skill in modern healthcare).

The realistic news? You're also in charge of making sure those relationships stay strong, which means managing expectations, handling complaints, and keeping people happy – without losing your mind. But there are considerations we can help you with, and hints on the types of things to be considered.

Think of how you created your business and marketing plan – that's the start of CRM – you're putting in place business practices that will put the practice in closer contact with patients. This allows learnings from each other and building value in the relationship. Fundamentally, you're influencing patient behavior through the actions of the practice – you do this with meaningful analysis and communication with the goal of patient movement toward, retention of, and value creation, for your practice. This means decreased use of practice resources, with higher revenue from the patient; for the patient, it's feeling better with needs being met.

Let's be clear about one thing – CRM *technology* is NOT CRM! CRM is not a technology; it's instead how you execute your business plan with respect to your patients in order to create mutual benefit. That means *using* technology – information technology (IT), information services (IS) – strategically to meet patient and practice needs. These need to be considered coincident – if it is just in one direction, for example, so that staff and providers never have to speak with patients – then it's

DOI: 10.4324/9781003685623-9

not a solution but a problem no matter how much practice resource you potentially are saving. But if you instead have a way for patients to pick appointment times from an open schedule online that allows them to fit into your clinic at a given time, with confirmation and a follow-up call – there's mutual benefit – THAT'S how CRM is supposed to work.

Medicine is a people business, and those people can be defined, as you did in the marketing exercise. By understanding that, you can obtain information ("data"). You walk the fine line of spending enough time creating a practice that will allow patients to feel that you're giving personal service, but at the same time, you need to effect an economy of scale by understanding those groups of patients who will provide your practice the most value, and who you in turn can meet their needs. Thus, there is a "front office" and "back office" component to this, and what CRM allows you to do is capture information that addresses both.

The operational side, or front office, is where sales and marketing and customer service – what you put in front of the patient – are housed, and the execution of the business plan. The back office is where you evaluate your patient base, and whether that's giving the practice value – are you spending enough time with the patients in the highest reimbursement groups; are you meeting the needs of this group; are you taking on too many patients with too many problems and/or too low of reimbursement; are you doing the things that avoid additional resources (e.g., denials), etc., and most importantly, are you getting feedback from the front office to the back office to ensure the needs of patients and the practice are being met? Thus, CRM is the package of how you interact with patients, how the patients interact with you, and how to maximize the value for each party with the business processes and systems you put in place.

Let's dive into how you can master the art of CRM in your solo private practice, with a little humor to keep things light (because, let's be honest, sometimes you'll need it).

## Step 1: The Warm Welcome (First Impressions Matter)

The front office is key to the practice, since that's where the first impression will occur. Now, the first impression may come from the electronic interface, or (even more importantly) how a patient first obtains information about the practice. For the latter, as part of your CRM, the first path to your door must be facile and available and easy to navigate for your target patients – if it's not, your CRM isn't working. Think about the pathway of referral to your practice. Is it the phone? Is it by internet presence? Is it through a shared electronic health record? Do you need paperwork filled out? Are those coming to see you only 20-year-olds who understand technology well, or are they middle aged or more senior who are less familiar with technology? You need to address your primary patient demographic while being flexible enough to encompass most of the patient types you will see. Forcing technology onto patients who are unwilling or unequipped for using it is poor implementation of CRM, no matter what the consultants tell you how much it will save the practice.

Remember, *any* patient interface is part of CRM – and as well, *again, medicine is a people business.* When your potential patients first call, are they put into an infinite loop of repetitive choices, or does a person actually answer the phone? If you receive an electronic referral through an electronic medical record, does someone actually monitor web traffic for potential patients trying to get in, or do inquiries go to an anonymous unmonitored email address? Not surprisingly, these have been CRM "solutions" that unwise IT/IS consultants who have never once spent time in the domain of medicine have put in place because it replaces people and ostensibly costs less. We have seen this and witnessed how practices have dwindled when high-value patients left because they were not willing to tolerate the hurdles, no matter how "good" the provider might have been (although, if the provider let this happen, maybe they weren't a great provider after all or was engulfed by a corporate machine).

Next, once the patient gets to the office, is there one receptionist with a line of patients waiting, as one by one, patients are processed? Or are there a number of reception staff constantly asking if they can help the patients coming into the office minimizing any wait? Has paperwork been requested previously of any new patients, either printable and handwritten or available online so those more savvy can have it entered already? Again, this is part of the CRM aspect of the practice. *Saving time and decreasing resource use is the key* – you want patients to come to your office, and limit the time with the paperwork, but you have to give options – which will provide you data on the *net value creation component of each patient*! Capturing those who spend less resources of the practice is key to know and helps create the other side of the coin – give more resource (e.g., availability) to those who spend less of the practices net resource. This is the backroom component. You've identified that these are the more valuable patients. That's not to say you won't see everyone, but you need to know who to prioritize with respect to everything from staff work to scheduling.

With that, you must obtain feedback from your patients about the processes you're implementing in order to make sure you're meeting both their needs and the practices. Part of the CRM rubric today is feedback, to a fault. One of us used to eschew the feedback loops that our practice had, and question the patient ourselves, and to a certain extent, still do so. But given that most patients are aware of the electronic medical record and can provide feedback, we let the patient know, as does the staff, that feedback is important since it allows us to do our job better. Again, this is the backroom stuff of data analysis – the more we get, the better we serve the patients and the practice. And of course, monitoring social media is a key component of the feedback cycle.

Think about your own experience, the last time you walked into a business and felt instantly comfortable. Maybe it was the aroma of freshly brewed coffee, the friendly greeting, or the way everything just felt effortless. That's the key – when we serve our patients, the last thing we want is to enter into the exam room with an unhappy, grumpy patient because of the barriers to entry they needed to jump over in order to arrive in the room with you. The CRM really does manifest as the value creating relationship between you as the provider and the patient, and the overall health of the practice. Better relationships between you and your patients portends better outcomes overall, even if and especially if the first thing you need to do is apologize. Human nature being what it is, often times that will assuage a situation. Again, that's all about CRM.

Now, think about a time when you walked into a business and immediately wanted to turn around and leave. How about a time when a business decided it was best to blame someone else for a product or service that was related to something you experienced. Did you feel fine with this? Did you just shrug your shoulders and attribute it up to the fates? And if this was a doctor's office, and the paperwork was lost, or the referral wasn't sent through, or you waited for an extra half/one/two hours since the provider was hopelessly behind and the staff were just sitting around and not giving updates, did you just note that you'd been in the same boat yourself? Is that the way you want your office to run? How do you think the patient reacted when the doctor walked in the room? Probably not the best of interactions.

Remember, your office, the staff, the *environs*, is your brand. It's the first thing a patient notices and experiences when they step through the door and *well before they get to you*. A well-lit, clean, and welcoming space sets the tone for their visit. A peeling linoleum floor and a surly receptionist who looks like she lost a bet to be there, not so much. This is all part of CRM, from the first interface by phone or electronically, the initial paperwork, entering into your office space, the staff's attitude, rooming the patient on time ... all before they get to you. Which patient would you like to see?

**Table 9.1 Front Office: Customer Facing Interactions**

| IT/IS in combination with in-person interface – correct ratios of each |
|---|
| New patient ease of obtaining appointments by phone and web-based interface |
| Ability to schedule appointments and provide timely information |
| Collection efficiency of copays/deductibles up front rather in arrears |

**Table 9.2 Back Office: Data Mining**

| Analytics: practice resource utilization by patients, reimbursement per given patient |
|---|
| Feedback/interpretation of feedback – waiting time, scheduling, collection delays, denial frequencies |
| Strategy development based on feedback and analysis |

There are software packages that can help with some of this, and there are services that can act as your telephone/internet front office. Use them wisely, but don't let them use you. Tables 9.1 and 9.2 suggest key issues for consideration when looking at CRM front and back-office solutions for your practice.

## Pro Tip: The Power of a Name

Dale Carnegie once said, "A person's name is, to that person, the sweetest sound in any language". Use it. Train your front desk staff to greet patients by name. If you don't have a front desk staff (welcome to solo practice!), then take a moment to do it yourself.

"Hi, Mrs. Thompson! How's that new grand-baby of yours?"

Boom.You just became her favorite doctor. And, if you take time to look at the baby pictures, you have just demonstrated to your patient that you care about more than the payment you are going to receive for that office visit.

## Step 2: Communication Is Everything

If there's one thing patients (or any of us) hate, it's being ignored. Whether it's waiting too long for an appointment, standing in a queue at your office, not understanding their test results, or feeling like they're talking to a brick wall, communication is key. This is, after all, the interface between the provider and patient, and how we personalize our services that creates the connection between us.

### *The 24-Hour Rule*

No, this isn't some obscure hospital protocol – it's a simple rule for solo practitioners: Respond to all patient inquiries within 24 hours. Whether it's a voicemail, an email, or a portal message, patients should never feel like they've been forgotten. If you can't get back to them personally, have a system in place (even if that system is a well-crafted email auto-response that says, "Dr. You is currently seeing patients but will respond within 24 hours"). Again, this is part of the CRM

**Table 9.3 Electronic CRM Components: Interface on Web and In-person at Office**

| |
|---|
| Scheduling into an online schedule with exit to speaking with live scheduler/online chat |
| Paperwork availability for download or online completion; provide incentives to patients to fill out (e.g., copies for other practices) |
| Communication to practice – as narrow (e.g.. MA) to broad (e.g., everyone, including provider) depending on what is considered appropriate to the practice |
| Patient alerts for appointments |
| Patient payments for copays/deductibles |
| Referral management including note transfer and patient information/scheduling |
| Patient feedback management |
| Insurance verification/authorization/eligibility (networks practice participates) |
| Ongoing insurance verification process |
| Patient education materials |
| Routing patient messages to staff/providers |

**Table 9.4 Telephony CRM Interfaces: Full Service**

| |
|---|
| Answers with practice name |
| Equipped with FAQs for answering commonly asked questions |
| Let the patient know the provider/surrogate will get back to the patient within 24 hours |
| Always asks for caller to provide feedback |
| Routes calls after inquiring if a live person can answer the phone – otherwise informs patient a message will be provided/can leave voicemail |
| Always asks for any other needs (e.g., patient education and prescriptions) before terminating call (always allows patient to terminate call first) |

aspect of electronic communication; staff as well need to manifest this level of communication. Our experiences may differ, particularly based on the type of communication permitted by the electronic medical record, but in general, having someone call the patient back if the provider is occupied should be part of the CRM protocol. Tables 9.3 and 9.4 give some additional aspects to consider when considering CRM interfaces and telephony.

## *Pro Tip: Explaining Things (Without Making Their Eyes Glaze Over)*

Patients appreciate doctors who take the time to explain things – but please, ditch the medical jargon. If you tell Mr. Williams that his hypertension is causing endothelial dysfunction, expect to see a blank stare (or worse, a Google search that convinces him he has six months to live). Instead, try:

> Your blood pressure is running high, and over time that can damage your blood vessels. But we can fix that with some lifestyle changes and maybe a little medication.

See? Simple. Clear. Reassuring.

## Step 3: The Art of Handling Complaints (Without Losing Your Cool)

Part of the CRM process is receiving feedback, and no matter even if you're an award-winning physician, you will get your share of complaints, which may be due to your receptionist or a stain in the carpet to you having a bad day. No matter how great you are, there will be complaints, but remember you're asking for feedback so you can get better. Now certainly there are those who may be irascible, but most of the time if there is an issue you can look upon it as an opportunity to get more data on *why*. Maybe a patient had to wait too long. Maybe they didn't like the treatment plan. Maybe they Googled their symptoms and are now convinced you missed their extremely rare tropical disease. Regardless, getting feedback provides information on what type(s) of patient(s) is/are unhappy, and more information can be garnered on their value to the practice.

Again, this is about the types of patients that utilize the practice resources considerably vs. those who don't – this is valuable to you as the business owner. An orthopedic surgeon we know was technically one of the best hand surgeons, and his bedside manner was just as good. He received a complaint online about his "poor performance" from an out-of-network patient who didn't think he did a good job examining her because he was left-handed! For those patients, additional resources are not worth expending. On the other hand, a neurologist we know had great diagnostic skills but did not do well explaining results to patients, and needed some coaching in simplification, to the benefit of both his patients and himself. That was a resource of time and money well-spent. Again, this is all part of how we interface with the patient, and the value we create for both parties.

Regardless, when faced with complaints, being defensive isn't of value. A suggestion is given below:
*The three-step complaint formula:*

1 Listen: Even if you're 99% sure they're wrong, let them talk. Sometimes, people just want to be heard.
2. Acknowledge and empathize: "I can see how that would be frustrating". (Notice you didn't say, *You're right!* Just that you understand.)
3 Offer a solution: "Here's what I can do to make this better for you".

Most complaints aren't about the actual problem – they're about feeling dismissed. Master the art of acknowledgment, and you'll turn frustrated patients into loyal ones. This is a key component of standard operating procedure of any practice not only for the provider, *but for* all *staff as well.* When one of us was at a first practice, we had a senior receptionist who was perceived by everyone as one of the nicest people anywhere – whenever there was a challenging situation, she always proactively went to speak with the patient/family/provider and virtually always diffused the situation. She was a great listener and never looked to blame anyone but always came up with a *next step solution.* As noted above, it's about creating a process of acknowledgment rather than finger-pointing that helps.

## Step 4: Loyalty and Retention: Creating Raving Fans

Good patient relationships don't just happen; they're built. The cycle of front-office operations, with back-office analysis from feedback and information, feeding to front-office operations again is a key component of building the business. If patients don't perceive you as a caring, understanding, and competent clinician, your practice may go the way of the dinosaurs. That's why the interfaces are so key– it's something we stress over and over again. There are certainly tactics for patient loyalty and retention (see below) but at its base, communication and responsiveness are the most relevant parts of customer service. That's why technology needs to be a *tool*, and not the CRM itself. The practices (and corporate agents) who have used the latter alone have fallen hard (look how many hospital practices lose millions of dollars a year!). A satisfied and loyal patient will not only return but will refer their friends, family, and even strangers at the grocery store to your practice (we've seen and heard it!).

## A Few Simple Ways to Build Patient Loyalty

*Follow-up calls*: A quick call after a procedure or a tough diagnosis makes a huge impact. ("Just checking in to see how you're feeling, Mr. Garcia".)

*A personal touch*: Remembering small details about their life ("How was your trip to Florida?") shows you see them as a person, not just a patient.

*A physical touch*: A handshake, a comforting hand on their shoulder, or even the passing of a tissue when tears are flowing shows you care about them as a person than just a diagnosis.

## Final Thoughts: CRM Is About Customer Service

Managing customer relations in a solo practice isn't about fancy software or corporate policies – it's about connection, communication, responsiveness – the bedrock of customer service. It's about making patients feel heard, valued, and cared for. But it is also about using the appropriate tools to allow the interface to be as value creating as possible, both for the patient and the practice. This includes understanding who are the highest value patients, and what are the barriers to meeting their needs as well as ensuring practice resources are being utilized in the most efficient way possible.

And let's be real – happy patients make your life easier. They follow treatment plans, they show up to appointments, and they don't write angry Yelp reviews about your waiting room music. In turn, your staff need to understand the customer service ethic and utilize the appropriate tools to serve the patients, rather than force unwieldy tools onto patients for the convenience of the staff and the practice. CRM operationalizes and captures why patients are happy and the practice is capturing value. Happy patients interacting with upbeat, encouraging staff minimizes the chance patients will be grouchy when you walk into the examination room.

CRM as a tool *helps us help our patients, and vice versa*. The best marketing strategy isn't necessarily an ad – rather, it's a patient who writes a glowing review on social media and tells their entire book club, "You HAVE to go see *my* doctor".

Because that's how great practices are built. One happy, value creating patient at a time.

# Chapter 10

# Personnel

## Introduction

When considering hiring staff for your practice, consider which roles require in-office personnel and which can be outsourced (see Chapter 9 for details). Your staffing needs will depend on several factors: whether you perform in-office procedures, use dedicated or shared space, and your overall practice model. The key is to consider all of these factors before you decide to hire, since as previously noted people are by far the most expensive part of any practice. Nonetheless, support staff can be essential, for example, particularly when your busy schedule prevents you from personally greeting patients promptly – a situation where having a receptionist becomes valuable.

## Considerations

As noted, personnel represent the largest expense in any organization. Beyond salaries and benefits, every employee – regardless of their position – requires management time and resources. While much has been written about the distinction between management and leadership, we won't delve into that debate here. Instead, recognize that your key responsibilities include: clearly defining objectives, communicating effectively, anticipating potential issues, motivating your team, and prioritizing operational tasks. We as clinical scientists can do a lot of these things, particularly with an analytical mindset derived from our various training(s). Also, being on a team through residency and fellowship helps us understand what does and doesn't motivate people. While some have noted that physicians make poor leaders, our experience suggests this is NOT the case, and that by refocusing on what we have experienced during training and, for some of us, in corporate medicine, we have the tools to be excellent managers and leaders.

One suggestion is that you make time in your schedule for nonclinical activities when you can review your business and operations. Also, create a *separate* time for yourself when you can catch


DOI: 10.4324/9781003685623-10

up on administrative work, and *only if absolutely necessary*, clinical work. The point is to have time set aside for nonclinical tasks, such as looking at, strategizing, and operationalizing business issues. Clinical issues are like a warm pie – they run over everything; you have to consciously set aside time to run the business and be sure you're looking out for your and the practice's future.

## Don't Leave It to Someone Else

It seems easy and straightforward to ask someone else to do both the hiring and run your practice. This is what corporate medicine seems to be – someone else – HR, finance, program management, medical directors, administrative "partners" (or whatever euphemism is used), etc. – "do" these activities, and all that is expected of us is to see the patients. While this certainly is what is being "sold", from experience the truth is much less sanguine. The tradeoff is that we become tools of "churn" – we're employees – being evaluated and directed to generate revenue for a corporation. While that is certainly reasonable, understand that this ties you to procedures, internal regulations and rules, working with bosses who are not skilled in the domain of medicine, as well as altering your perspective and freedom to practice the way you might want, notwithstanding taking a cut in pay. For some, the price is right, and there is a willingness to accept these conditions. For others, more independence and compensation are desired.

Hence, the advantage of doing your own hiring is that you're hiring the people you want to work with. Again, as mentioned previously, our strong suggestion is to hire for personality and train for skills; as long as your employees have the motivation and the intelligence to do the job right, they're far better than the reverse. If you leave the hiring to someone else, they may hire on the basis of job qualifications alone, and that's NOT what you want to do – your time is the most important resource, and management of people takes time – even good people – and management of bad people with poor attitudes takes way, way more time! You want to have employees you like, who can either learn or have already learned, and that you're confident can perform when the chips are down.

## Have a Process

As noted before, it's very important to have both a process for hiring as well as a practice handbook that sets out the rules and regulations of the practice ("SOPs", i.e., standard operating procedures from Chapter 4). Our advice is to get these from the legal or practice consultants on your team or download them from the internet, as noted in Chapter 4. In any event, do this before you start looking for staff so you have something to reference when you start doing interviews. In this rubric, you should have not only the SOPs but also a job description. You also want to decide how you will access resumes (usually by web-based means), the number of references you expect, and how/when you will interview candidates. For those applicants who are acceptable, undergoing background checks and confirming qualifications completes the initial interview screen, while providing an offer, with negotiation (see Chapter 7), finalizes the process.

## Benefits

Benefits are something that larger practices tend to offer. Smaller practices may or may not offer benefits, depending on the type of practice, and whether you have personnel that require them.

Even corporate practices don't automatically provide benefits, and in some of the largest practices in the country, you may not get benefits if your spouse already receives them! Moreover, your spouse may *not* receive benefits either if they don't "fit" the requirements the corporation has for a spouse! One of us experienced both of these scenarios – it's not a rare occurrence. In general, providing benefits such as medical insurance subsidies, vacation, and 401k allows you to decrease salary a bit and is a marketing tool; not providing benefits suggests you pay a bit more. We've found our insurance brokers as well as online job boards provide a wealth of information about customary pay and benefits in the local area. As we've previously articulated in this book, none of this requires you to go in blind without information.

## Skin in the Game

Depending on the type of practice you have, motivation is key to having employees who feel appreciated and want to do the best for your practice. As well, they want to do the best for themselves. Hence, in certain cases you can motivate employees by giving them incentives. For an aesthetic practice we're familiar with, any sales above a certain amount per month goes directly to the staff member selling the products; not unexpectedly the customer service and sales for that practice are very high. Another primary care practice we know about provides a certain percentage back to all the staff at the end of the quarter if the spending is less than budget (with a small celebratory lunch). Being creative (and rigorous) about providing everyone the motivation to collect more revenues and decrease the overall spend allows for better office morale when successful, and a "we're in this together" view, particularly when things get tight and cost-containment efforts need to be more stringent. If you think about your own experiences, you'll see this isn't so far afield from what any of us need to feel appreciated and motivated toward performing well.

## The Office Manager

This position is particularly relevant within a practice, if it's not you who's playing that role. Many solo-preneurs/solo-practitioners function as their own office managers (OMs), particularly when they are first starting in practice, whether they come directly from a training program or from a group/corporate practice. The key is to utilize the information available in this book and other sources to run the business and the practice with an assembled outsourced team, as well as do the clinical work in an efficient manner. Both of us have experienced the solo and the OM models, and both can be successful, if the person who plays the role of OM works well with the head clinical person (you!).

For those who want to have an OM, all of the aforementioned information is relevant. A good OM is worth the time they are saving you from dealing with administrative details that you no longer need to be *directly* involved with (but you still need to be involved with thorough oversight). Giving the OM incentives is even more important than the rest of the staff, since they will be responsible for ensuring everything stays on budget, costs are kept down, and staff are motivated. You can see how the OM can make or break you and your practice, so take your time and vet prior to hiring this individual.

The OM is overseen by you, and as part of the time you are spending overseeing the practice, you need to oversee and manage them. If you have more staff than just an OM, the OM is managing the staff (as you are, but more at an arm's length) and you are directly managing the OM. You need to communicate your vision and objectives to everyone, but particularly to the OM to ensure understanding. Also, you need to meet with the OM regularly. Don't succumb to just handing the practice over to the OM – you'll regret it when mistakes happen that cause implications so egregious that Herculean efforts are required to dig out (see *MIT Beer Game*)! Remember, this is *your* practice – you write all the checks, you make all the revenue – don't give up your role unless you are willing to take the risk of living with someone else's decisions.

When you meet with the OM, ensure you have a regular agenda. In our experience, personnel, profit and loss statement, vendor management, billing/receiving, and denial updates are key to assess, as well as time for other issues that don't strictly fall under those categories. Trust, but verify what you're being told, and like with mid-levels, you want to be sure the assessment and plan truly reflect the data in front of you.

Finally, *be willing to be educated by the OM.* You should be able to do everything in the practice like you did in residency/fellowship, from writing orders to ordering supplies. The reason for this is obviously that you never want to over-depend on someone else, since this is your practice. While you can't do everything, being able to troubleshoot when things go awry certainly can save you time and money in the short and long term. Since the OM's job is to be detail oriented, they may know things on a logistic scale you don't – get educated! Your profitability and thus your patients depend on it.

## Keeping It Legal

Your consultant team will be able to advise you on what you need to do for hiring. Suffice to say it's primarily about legal requirements and paying taxes. Further, as an employer, you need to comply with the occupational safety and health act, as well as keep records. Your accounting and legal team can help you set this up. Table 10.1 lists the most relevant aspects.

**Table 10.1 Requirements for Hiring Employees**

| |
|---|
| 1. Set up EIN |
| 2. Keep record of employment taxes |
| Federal income tax withholdings |
| Federal wage and tax statements |
| State tax regulations |
| 3. Employee verification (I-9) |
| 4. Report hires to state directory |
| 5. Set up workers' compensation insurance |
| 6. Post required federal and state required notifications |
| 7. Consult IRS tax guide/accountant to assess when you need to file taxes |
| 8. Set up record keeping on: |
| Tax |
| Laboratory |
| Occupational safety and Health Act Compliance |
| Employment law |
| Standards that protect employee rights |

# Chapter 11

# Navigating Credentialing and Payor Contracts

## Introduction

Many physicians complete their residency or leave corporate medicine with exceptional clinical skills but find themselves unprepared for the administrative journey that is medical credentialing and payor contracting. Yet these processes form the very foundation of your private practice's financial viability if you decide to take payment from third-party payors. Handled strategically, they create steady revenue streams; managed poorly, they can doom your practice before the first patient walks through your door.

We're going to demystify the complex world of credentialing and payor contracts, providing you with a roadmap for launching your private practice with strong reimbursement fundamentals. While clinical excellence may be your passion, mastering these business aspects is essential to creating a sustainable practice where you can deliver that excellence for years to come.

## Part I: Understanding Credentialing – The Gateway to Reimbursement

### *What Is Credentialing?*

Credentialing is the process of verifying your qualifications, experience, practice history, malpractice insurance, and other critical information. This validation occurs at multiple levels: with insurance companies to join their provider networks, hospitals for admitting privileges, surgery centers for procedure privileges, and Medicare and Medicaid for participation in government programs.

 DOI: 10.4324/9781003685623-11

Think of credentialing as building your professional identity in the healthcare ecosystem. Without it, you cannot bill insurance companies, admit patients to hospitals, or participate in most insurance networks. It's your ticket to doing business in the healthcare world. Regardless of what type of practice you do, credentialing is required in all facets (corporate or otherwise).

## *The Timeline Reality Check*

Perhaps the most crucial aspect of credentialing to understand is its timeline. Many physicians make the catastrophic mistake of assuming credentialing will take a few weeks. The reality is far different. Typical credentialing timelines are much longer than most new practitioners expect. Insurance panels typically take 90–180 days, hospital privileges need about 60–120 days, Medicare enrollment requires 60–90 days, Medicaid enrollment can range from 60 to 180 days depending on your state, and even your DEA registration will take 30–60 days.

Here's our most strategic planning point: Begin your credentialing process at least six months before your planned practice opening date (see Timeline). If you're transitioning from an existing practice, initiate credentialing processes the moment you decide to make the change. Too many physicians are left unable to bill for services because they underestimated these timelines.

## *Building Your Credentialing Dossier*

Before applying to a single entity, assemble a comprehensive credentialing dossier containing all required documentation. This preparation will streamline applications and reduce delays.

Your essential dossier again are the standard documents you'll need for any practice environment. If you've come from another practice, you'll recognize these aspects; as well, if you've transitioned from residency to a fellowship program at another institution, this will also look familiar. The components should include the following:

1. Your medical degree and diploma in official copies
2. Residency and fellowship certificates
3. Board certification documentation
4. Current state medical license(s)
5. DEA registration/state-controlled substance license if applicable
6. Current CV including work history with no gaps in timeline (and explanations for any gaps over 30 days)
7. Malpractice insurance declarations page with proof of malpractice history or claims history reports
8. National Provider Identifier documentation
9. Professional references (typically 3)
10. Practice information, including address, tax ID, phone/fax, hospital affiliations and privileges, and immunization records.

Here's a practical tip: Create both digital and physical "credentialing binders" containing these documents. Maintain scanned color copies of all originals at 300 DPI or higher quality. You'll be surprised how often you'll need to access these documents, and having them organized from the start will save countless hours.

## The CAQH ProView System: Your Central Hub

The Council for Affordable Quality Healthcare (CAQH) ProView system functions as a centralized repository for your credentials. It can be accessed here: www.caqh.org/providers. Most commercial insurers use this platform, allowing you to enter your information once and share it with multiple payors.

For CAQH best practices, complete your profile thoroughly, leaving no fields blank (use "N/A" if truly not applicable). Update your profile quarterly at minimum. You will need to re-attest every 120 days, but this can either be done by a surrogate or at your convenience. Typically you will receive a reminder to do this by email. Upload all supporting documents in the specified format. Check the "global authorization" option to allow all participating insurers access.

One of the most common CAQH pitfalls we see is letting your CAQH attestation expire. This simple oversight can add months to your insurance enrollment timelines. Don't let this happen to you!

## Medicare Enrollment Essentials

Enrolling as a Medicare provider involves navigating the Provider Enrollment, Chain, and Ownership System (PECOS). This process deserves special attention given Medicare's importance to most practices. Here is a link to the PECOS website: https://pecos.cms.hhs.gov/pecos/login.do#headingLv1

You have several Medicare enrollment options. You can enroll as an individual provider (Part B) for solo practitioners billing under their own NPI, as a group practice using a group NPI and tax ID, as participating vs. non-participating (which determines whether you accept assignment for Medicare claims), or you can opt out by formally withdrawing from Medicare (which requires patient contracts).

There are critical Medicare deadlines you must be aware of. You must enroll within 30 days of your practice start date to avoid retroactive billing restrictions. We suggest you start six months before your practice start date. Revalidation is required every 3–5 years, and changes to practice information must be reported within 30 days.

Here's a strategic consideration: For most specialists, Medicare patients represent 20–40% of a typical practice. Carefully consider the financial implications before deciding to opt out of Medicare, particularly in specialties serving older populations. Some physicians make this decision without fully understanding the impact on their patient base and revenue.

## Medicaid Enrollment Considerations

Medicaid enrollment processes vary dramatically by state but generally involve more paperwork and longer timelines than Medicare enrollment.

Key Medicaid variables by state include application processes (which may be paper vs. online), supporting documentation requirements, site visit requirements, fingerprinting and background check processes, and revalidation timelines (typically 3–5 years).

When it comes to Medicaid participation strategy, in some regions and specialties, Medicaid participation may be financially challenging due to low reimbursement rates. However, many *managed* Medicaid plans offer significantly better rates than traditional Medicaid. Consider enrolling with these managed plans even if you limit traditional Medicaid participation. Again, as noted in earlier chapters, ensuring you know what levels of reimbursement you receive per payor allows you an understanding of which groups of patients to prioritize in your practice.

### Hospital Privileges and Credentialing

Hospital credentialing processes vary by institution but typically involve detailed application forms, verification of all credentials, peer references, background checks, review by credentials committee and medical executive committee, and board approval.

For hospital strategy, apply for privileges at all hospitals where you anticipate needing to provide care. For specialists, this includes hospitals where you might receive referrals. For primary care, consider hospitals where you would refer patients. A side note – be careful on the number of hospitals you decide to apply for privileges; some hospitals charge for application, and you don't want to have to admit patients all over town since you don't get paid for traveling from hospital to hospital.

Most hospitals require procedure logs demonstrating your experience with specific procedures. Maintain detailed logs during residency and fellowship to facilitate this process, or if you haven't done this, you can request the billing part of your training institution to be able to provide it to you. Failing to keep or have these logs can result in you having to jump through extraordinary hoops to document your experience retroactively.

### Credentialing Verification Organizations (CVOs)

CVOs specialize in managing the credentialing process for healthcare providers, offering services ranging from application completion to tracking and follow-up.

You might want to consider a CVO when opening a new practice with multiple providers, expanding to multiple locations, joining numerous insurance panels simultaneously, or if you lack in-house credentialing expertise.

From a cost consideration perspective, CVOs typically charge $400–$1000 per provider, depending on services needed. While this represents an upfront cost, the potential revenue protected by avoiding credentialing delays often justifies the expense. The return on investment (ROI) on these services can be substantial, especially for specialized practices.

## Part II: Mastering Payor Contracts – Securing Your Financial Future

### The Contract Landscape Overview

Payor contracts establish the legal and financial relationship between your practice and insurance companies. These contracts determine reimbursement rates for services, payment timelines, administrative requirements, audit and review processes, and term and termination provisions.

Here's a critical insight many miss: Many physicians mistakenly assume all insurance contracts are non-negotiable. In reality, almost every aspect of these agreements can be negotiated, particularly for specialties in high demand in your market. Don't leave money on the table by accepting the first offer!

## Identifying Priority Payors for Your Practice

*Not all insurance contracts hold equal value for your practice.* Prioritize your contracting efforts based on market research factors. Consider the dominant insurers in your geographic area, patient insurance demographics in your specialty, employer-sponsored plans in your region, exchange plans with significant market share, and Medicare Advantage penetration rates.

To collect this essential data, request payor mix reports from colleagues in your specialty, ask referral sources about their patients' insurance distribution, contact your local medical society for regional insurance data, and review healthcare market reports for your area. *If you've been in a practice in the past in the local area, and/or done training, this information is readily available from the billing group with whom you've already worked.*

For strategic sequencing, approach the highest volume payors first but be cautious about neglecting smaller ones that might serve specific patient populations important to your practice. Some specialists build successful practices by strategically contracting with niche insurers that larger groups ignore.

## Understanding Fee Schedules and Reimbursement Methodologies

The fee schedule attached to your contract is arguably its most important component, yet many physicians sign contracts without fully understanding the reimbursement structure. As noted in other parts of this book, READ. YOUR. CONTRACTS. (and understand them!).

You'll encounter several common reimbursement methodologies. Some payors use a percentage of Medicare, setting rates as a percentage of the Medicare Physician Fee Schedule (e.g., 110% of Medicare). Others use Resource-Based Relative Value Scale (RBRVS), with payments based on relative value units (RVUs) with a conversion factor. You might see case rates or global payments, which provide a single payment covering all services for a specific condition or procedure. Traditional fee-for-service schedules offer payor-specific rates for each service. And some plans use capitation, providing a fixed per-member-per-month payment regardless of services provided (*avoid these contracts at all costs* – these are resource draining and are ones of diminishing returns).

Here's a conversion factor alert worth considering: Two contracts both offering "120% of Medicare" might pay quite differently if they use different Medicare base years or conversion factors. Always clarify which year's Medicare schedule is being referenced. Practices can lose significant revenue by missing this detail.

## Fee Schedule Analysis and Modeling

Before signing any contract, model its financial impact on your practice. First, identify your most commonly performed procedures (by CPT code). Determine the anticipated volume for each code. You should easily be able to ascertain both of these based on your residency/fellowship volumes and/or what you want to see, or what you've seen if you've already been in practice. Calculate expected reimbursement under the proposed fee schedule. Compare to your projected costs for delivering these services. And establish a minimum acceptable reimbursement threshold.

Here's a practical approach we recommend: Create a spreadsheet with your top CPT codes, their volumes, and a side-by-side comparison of proposed rates across different payors. This visualization makes contract value immediately apparent and helps you focus your negotiation efforts.

## *Contract Red Flags and Negotiation Priorities*

Not all concerning contract provisions relate to fee schedules. Luckily, billing and reimbursement consultants are well-aware of these issues and can help look at your contracts and assess for these aspects. Key red flags for you to watch out for:

1. Problematic clauses like "unilateral amendment", which are provisions that allow the payor to change terms without your consent.
2. Be wary of all-products clauses that force participation in all of a payor's insurance products.
3. Silent PPO arrangements allow discount sharing with other entities.
4. Ambiguous medical necessity definitions give payors broad discretion to deny claims.
5. Unreasonable timely filing limits restrict your ability to submit claims.
6. Onerous chart audit provisions allow excessive documentation reviews.
7. Noncompete or exclusivity requirements limit your ability to contract with others; these are fortunately less common given antitrust regulations being developed.
8. Undefined "quality" metrics tie reimbursement to unspecified measures.

While fee schedules naturally receive the most attention, these administrative provisions often have equal long-term impact on your practice's viability. Some physicians focus exclusively on rates, only to be hamstrung by administrative requirements that dramatically increase their overhead costs.

## *Effective Contract Negotiation Strategies*

Negotiating with insurance companies requires preparation, persistence, and strategy. We discuss negotiating in depth in Chapter 7.

Your greatest leverage often comes from your willingness to remain out-of-network if terms are unfavorable (i.e., your "BATNA" – best alternative to a negotiated agreement – again, see Chapter 7). This position is strengthened when you have strong patient relationships, unique services, or high demand for your specialty. Some specialists successfully secure rates 30% higher than initial offers by strategically leveraging their market position.

## *Understanding Value-Based Contracts and Alternative Payment Models*

As healthcare transitions from fee-for-service to value-based care, your contracting strategy must evolve. You'll encounter common value-based structures like pay-for-performance (P4P) with bonuses for meeting quality metrics, shared savings programs that allow participation in cost reduction with shared benefits, bundled payments that provide a single payment for an episode of care, risk-bearing arrangements where you accept downside risk for cost overruns, and direct primary care models that offer patient membership outside insurance. Coding and billing courses and consultants are quite familiar with these evolutions, but all providers would do well to understand these, no matter what type of practice is undertaken.

When evaluating these contracts, independently and/or with your billing and coding group, assess risk adjustment methodologies, quality metric validity and reliability, your ability to influence the measured outcomes, data reporting requirements and costs, and potential upside vs. downside risk. Once you've become familiar with the context, you'll see what most contracts are trying to accomplish is minimizing multiple payment provisions and replacing them with ones where a given outcome is associated with a given payment. Knowing what you need to get what you're being paid for, and what you aren't, is the key parameter to evaluate.

Our strategic implementation advice: Consider starting with upside-only arrangements before accepting downside risk, allowing your practice to develop the necessary care management infrastructure. Some practices rush into risk arrangements before building proper infrastructure, with disastrous financial consequences.

### Medicare Advantage and Managed Medicaid Contracting

These government program derivatives deserve special contracting attention. For Medicare Advantage, remember that rates are typically negotiable despite government program status. These plans often include quality incentive opportunities but may have more restrictive networks than traditional Medicare and often require prior authorizations not found in traditional Medicare.

With Managed Medicaid, these plans often pay significantly better than fee-for-service Medicaid, may offer incentive programs for patient engagement, typically have specific social determinants of health programs, and often have unique reporting requirements.

Our strategic approach recommendation: Consider these programs as *commercial* insurance products with unique regulatory overlays rather than as direct government programs. Negotiate accordingly.

### Out-of-Network and Cash-Pay Strategies

Some practices deliberately remain out-of-network with certain payors or operate entirely on a cash basis. Out-of-network considerations include potential for higher reimbursement per service, greater clinical autonomy, reduced administrative burden, and risk of patient financial responsibility.

Cash practice models include direct primary care memberships, concierge models, time-of-service discounted payment, package pricing for common services, and subscription models for ongoing care.

Many successful practices maintain in-network status with major payors while remaining out-of-network with lower-paying plans, creating a balanced revenue model. Many practices thrive with this hybrid approach, carefully selecting which plans warrant in-network participation.

## Implementing Effective Systems and Workflows

### Creating a Credentialing Calendar and Tracking System

Systematic tracking prevents costly credentialing lapses. Your tracking components should include application submission dates, follow-up schedules (typically every 2–3 weeks), document expiration dates, revalidation deadlines, and contact information for each payor's credentialing department.

Technology options include dedicated credentialing software, practice management system modules, custom spreadsheet systems, and credentialing service providers.

This is a critical process: Assign clear ownership of the credentialing tracking system to a specific team member in the practice if you have employees, with regular reporting to you. Without accountability, critical deadlines can be missed. If you are doing it yourself, set a reminder on your calendar to ensure this is tracked and you are reminded.

## *Ongoing Credentialing Maintenance*

Credentialing is not a one-time task but an ongoing process. Regular maintenance tasks include license renewal tracking, board certification monitoring, DEA registration renewal, CAQH attestation updates, Medicare and Medicaid revalidation, malpractice insurance renewal coordination, and hospital privilege renewals.

We recommend a systematic approach. Create a master calendar with email alerts for approaching deadlines, building in adequate lead time for document gathering and submission. Alternatively, CAQH will inform you of the need for updating your documents. If you don't pay attention to deadlines, you can lose the ability to bill for weeks or months due to missed renewal deadlines. Fortunately, once set up, reminders will typically be recurring.

## *Contract Management Systems*

As your practice grows, so does the complexity of managing multiple payor agreements. Management components include contract anniversary and renewal dates, fee schedule comparison tools, and key provision summaries.

Consider technology solutions like contract management software, secure digital storage with optical character recognition capabilities, automated renewal reminder systems, and fee schedule analysis tools. Your billing people will also have ways to address this as well and certainly are paid to do so. With growing contract numbers, it is wise to very much consider a billing service that can accommodate your needs.

## *Fee Schedule Analysis Tools*

Fee schedule analysis tools are essential resources for physicians venturing into private practice, yet many practitioners overlook their importance until revenue falls short of expectations. Let's walk you through why these tools matter and how they can transform your practice's financial health.

First, these tools function as your practice's financial compass, providing clarity in the often murky waters of medical billing. These sophisticated platforms allow you to compare your fees against Medicare rates, regional averages, and specialty-specific benchmarks. Rather than setting prices in the dark, you'll see exactly how your fees stack up against the market.

Second, the real power of these tools lies in their contract modeling capabilities. Before walking into negotiations with insurance companies, you can simulate different fee scenarios and understand their impact on your bottom line. Imagine knowing precisely what a 10% increase in your top five procedure codes would mean for your annual revenue, or being able to calculate whether accepting a new insurance contract would be profitable based on your specific patient mix.

Third, beyond simple fee comparison, these platforms provide insights into your practice's utilization patterns. They highlight which procedures generate the most revenue, where your time is best spent, and which services might be underutilized.

The marketplace offers several robust options. CodeCorrect provides exceptional Medicare benchmarking, while FeeScout specializes in specialty-specific optimization. Many practices find Healthcare Compliance Pros valuable for its combined focus on compliance and comparative data. For those just starting out, the fee analysis features built into your practice management system may suffice initially, though they typically lack the depth of standalone solutions.

Implementation requires some upfront investment of time – you'll need to export data from your billing system and map your procedure codes to the analysis tool – but the ROI is typically substantial. Most practices discover fee adjustment opportunities that increase revenue by 5–8% or more within the first year, often without seeing additional patients.

As you build your private practice, remember that clinical excellence and business savvy must go hand in hand. Fee schedule analysis tools provide the data-driven insights that transform gut feelings into strategic decisions. In a healthcare landscape where margins continually tighten, this technology offers a clear advantage in sustaining a thriving practice that serves both your patients and your financial well-being. Again, using this along with your billing service will garner maximal revenue capture as your practice grows.

For operational integration, ensure your practice management software correctly reflects current contract terms and fee schedules for accurate revenue projections. Practices frequently leave money on the table if their billing systems weren't updated with current contracted rates.

### Payor Relations Strategy

Developing ongoing relationships with payor representatives facilitates problem resolution. For relationship development, identify and record *key contacts at each payor*, schedule periodic check-in calls or meetings, address minor issues promptly before escalation, share quality improvement initiatives, and participate in payor provider advisory groups when available.

We recommend a diplomatic approach: Maintain professional relationships even through disagreements. The representative who helps resolve today's denied claim might be crucial for next year's contract negotiation. Practices that maintain good payor relationships often are able to successfully resolve issues that similarly situated practices could not.

## Special Considerations for Different Practice Types

### Solo Practice Special Considerations

Solo practitioners face unique challenges and opportunities. Credentialing challenges include managing the process without dedicated staff, potentially longer processing times, and greater impact from any credentialing delays.

Contract considerations include potentially less negotiating leverage (if practicing in a low-demand specialty), the importance of specialty societies for contract guidance, critical need for thorough financial modeling, and value of joining Independent Physician Associations (IPAs).

Our strategic approach recommendation for solo practitioners: Consider credentialing assistance services for the initial setup, then develop simplified maintenance systems manageable by limited staff. The investment in initial professional help often pays dividends through faster enrollment and better contracts.

### Hospital-Affiliated Practice Considerations

Practices closely affiliated with hospitals have unique considerations. Professional Services Agreements (PSAs) may include credentialing support, may come with pre-negotiated payor rates, typically include specific quality and volume expectations, and may limit independent contracting opportunities.

Alignment considerations include potential for "leakage" penalties for out-of-network referrals, coordination with hospital contracting departments, access to hospital-negotiated rates, and participation requirements in hospital quality programs.

We suggest a strategic balance: Understand both the benefits and limitations of hospital alignment when it comes to payor relationships and credentialing support. The security of hospital-negotiated rates comes with trade-offs in autonomy that should be carefully weighed.

### *Telemedicine Credentialing and Contracting*

Telemedicine may present distinct credentialing and contracting challenges. Multistate considerations include Interstate Medical Licensure Compact (IMLC) (https://imlcc.com/a-faster-pathway-to-physician-licensure/) participation, state-specific telemedicine requirements, varied credentialing processes for virtual care, and location-specific reimbursement policies. Luckily, with the IMLC and efforts to create parity among states, the homogeneity on requirements between states has increased for those in the compact. One of us has literally started seeing patients by telemedicine where a license through IMLC took only about ten days! While not every state is part of the IMLC, almost 40 are, and telemedicine has become a viable alternative for practitioners in many different subspecialties today. However, be wary that telemedicine contract provisions may specify technology requirements and standards, documentation specifications, and virtual care payment parity provisions with provider responsibility.

For expansion strategy, when expanding telemedicine across state lines, prioritize states with streamlined licensing processes and strong payment parity laws. Practices can strategically sequence their multistate expansion to maximize revenue while minimizing administrative burden.

## Navigating Common Challenges and Pitfalls

### *Addressing Credentialing Denials and Delays*

When credentialing problems arise, systematic troubleshooting is essential. Common reasons for denial include incomplete applications, malpractice history concerns, network adequacy limitations, board certification requirements, missing or inconsistent information, and practice history gaps.

Strategies for resolving denials include requesting specific reason for denial in writing, addressing issues directly rather than resubmitting blindly, escalating to network management when appropriate, considering appeal processes outlined by the payor, and documenting all communications regarding the denial, including the date of the communication and the name of the person you communicated with.

Our prevention strategy recommendation: Conduct a thorough self-assessment of any potential red flags in your application before submission and proactively address them with supporting documentation. Physicians with complex histories can secure credentialing by proactively explaining past issues rather than hoping they wouldn't be discovered.

### *Managing Network Closure Challenges*

Many desirable insurance networks close to new providers. Navigate these barriers with access strategies. Demonstrate unique services unavailable in-network, highlight specialized training or procedures, provide evidence of patient access issues, and show geographic coverage gaps in the existing network.

We recommend a persistence protocol: Network status can change quarterly. Implement a regular reapplication schedule (typically every 3–6 months) for closed networks that are priorities for your practice. Persistent physicians can eventually gain access to networks that initially denied them.

### *Contract Termination and Renegotiation*

When contract terms become untenable, strategic termination and renegotiation may be necessary. Termination considerations include contract notification periods (typically 90–180 days), patient notification requirements, continuity of care provisions for existing patients, potential network adequacy mandates in your state, and impact on hospital relationships and referral patterns.

For renegotiation timing, initiate discussions 6–9 months before renewal dates, present data supporting requested changes, be prepared with market comparison information, and consider phased implementation of significant changes.

Develop a patient communication plan with templates for patient notification that comply with contractual and legal requirements while preserving your professional relationships. The way you communicate network changes to patients can significantly impact retention.

### *Adapting to Payor Policy Changes*

Insurance companies frequently change policies affecting reimbursement. Therefore, utilizing monitoring systems can help you remain current with these changes. Subscribe to payor newsletters and updates, join specialty society payor policy committees, regularly review payor provider portals, and implement coding update services.

Your responses to insurance company policy changes can include impact analysis for significant changes, staff education on new requirements, EHR template modifications for documentation changes, and financial projection updates.

When policy changes violate contract terms, prepare formal appeals with specific contract references and proposed resolutions. Practices can successfully challenge policy changes by demonstrating contractual violations.

## Building Your Credentialing and Contracting Team

### *Key Team Roles and Responsibilities*

Effective credentialing and contracting requires clear responsibility assignment. Essential roles include a credentialing coordinator who manages application processes and tracking, a contract analyst who reviews and compares contract terms and fee schedules, a billing manager who ensures contracts are correctly implemented in billing systems, a clinical documentation specialist who aligns provider documentation with contract requirements, and a practice manager/administrator who oversees the entire process and makes strategic decisions.

Even in small practices, clearly delineate these responsibilities among available staff to prevent oversight of critical functions. You don't need separate people for each role, but you do need clarity about who handles what. As well, be clear what activities are outsourced, and those which remain in-house. For one of us, much of these issues were outsourced initially and then subsequently underwent a hybrid approach as the practice grew.

Specialized training for staff handling these functions typically delivers substantial return through improved contract terms and reduced credentialing delays. The investment in staff training pay for itself many times over. *N.B.* See next section whether to do this in-house or outsource.

### *When to Outsource vs. Handle In-House*

The decision to outsource or manage these functions internally depends on several factors. Outsourcing considerations include practice size and complexity, staff expertise and availability, credentialing volume and frequency, contract negotiation confidence, and budget constraints.

Hybrid approaches worth considering include outsourcing initial credentialing while building internal maintenance capacity, handling routine contracts in-house while engaging experts for major negotiations, and using consultants for system setup, then managing ongoing processes internally.

Compare the fully loaded cost of internal staffing (salary, benefits, training, systems) against outsourced options, considering both direct costs and opportunity costs of potential delays or suboptimal contracts. Sometimes what seems more expensive is actually more economical when all factors are considered.

## Future Trends in Credentialing and Contracting

### *Digital Transformation in Credentialing*

The credentialing landscape is evolving with new technologies. These include online verification of credentials, centralized primary source verification, real-time license and certification monitoring, automated expiration management, and integration with provider directories.

Stay informed about these developments through professional organizations and be prepared to adapt your processes as new technologies become standard. The early adopters of these technologies often gain efficiency advantages over competitors.

### *Evolving Reimbursement Models*

The shift from volume to value continues to reshape contracting. New reimbursement models include direct employer contracting, reference-based pricing arrangements, consumer-directed healthcare approaches, social determinants of health incentives, and total cost of care arrangements.

Begin developing the infrastructure (care management, data analytics, quality reporting) needed to succeed in these models even while fee-for-service remains dominant. Forward-thinking practices can secure advantageous positions in their markets by preparing early for these shifts.

## Conclusion: From Administrative Burden to Strategic Advantage

While credentialing and contracting can initially appear as administrative hurdles, they represent crucial strategic opportunities for your practice. Approached with the right systems, knowledge, and mindset, these processes establish the financial foundation that allows your clinical excellence to flourish.

The physicians who thrive in private practice recognize that mastering these business elements isn't a distraction from medicine – it's what makes the practice of medicine sustainable on your own terms. By investing appropriate time and resources in these foundational elements, you create a practice that can deliver both excellent patient care and appropriate financial rewards.

*As you build your practice, remember that credentialing opens the door to seeing patients, but contracts determine what happens financially once they walk through that door.* Both deserve your careful attention as you create a practice that will sustain you throughout your career.

Take these action steps today: Create your credentialing dossier with all required documentation. Develop a timeline working backward from your planned practice opening date (see Figure 4.1). Identify the top five payors in your area for initial contracting focus. Determine whether to handle credentialing in-house or outsource. Begin researching typical contract terms for your specialty in your region.

With strategic planning and systematic execution, you can navigate the complex world of credentialing and contracting successfully, creating a strong foundation for your private practice journey. Countless physicians have done exactly that, and we know you can too.

## Private Practice Launch Checklist: Credentialing and Payor Contracts

### Credentialing Preparation (6+ months before opening)

[ ] Create comprehensive credentialing dossier with all required documentation
[ ] Prepare both digital and physical "credentialing binders"
[ ] Assemble medical degree and diplomas (official copies)
[ ] Gather residency and fellowship certificates
[ ] Collect board certification documentation
[ ] Ensure current state medical license(s) are in order
[ ] Verify DEA registration/state-controlled substance license status
[ ] Update CV
[ ] Obtain malpractice insurance declarations page and claims history reports
[ ] Document National Provider Identifier information
[ ] Secure professional references
[ ] Compile practice information (address, tax ID, phone/fax, hospital affiliations)

### Credential Platform Setup

[ ] Complete CAQH ProView profile comprehensively
[ ] Set calendar reminders for quarterly CAQH updates and 120-day re-attestations
[ ] Upload all supporting documents in specified format
[ ] Check "global authorization" option for insurance access
[ ] Begin Medicare enrollment through PECOS
[ ] Determine Medicare participation strategy (individual provider, group practice, participating vs. non-participating)
[ ] Research state-specific Medicaid enrollment requirements and timeline

### Hospital and Facility Privileges

[ ] Identify key hospitals/facilities for your practice

[ ] Gather and organize procedure logs from residency/fellowship
[ ] Apply for privileges at selected facilities
[ ] Create tracking system for application status at each facility

**Payor Contract Analysis**

[ ] Identify dominant insurers in your geographic area
[ ] Create prioritized list of payors for contracting efforts

**Fee Schedule Analysis**

[ ] Identify your ten most commonly performed procedures by CPT code
[ ] Create spreadsheet for side-by-side fee schedule comparison
[ ] Establish minimum acceptable reimbursement thresholds
[ ] Investigate fee schedule analysis tools (CodeCorrect, FeeScout, Healthcare Compliance Pros)

**Contract Negotiation Preparation**

[ ] Review contract red flags (unilateral amendment clauses, all-products clauses, etc.)
[ ] Determine your BATNA (Best Alternative to a Negotiated Agreement)
[ ] Assess your market leverage (unique services, specialty demand)
[ ] Develop strategy for value-based payment models
[ ] Consider out-of-network and cash-pay approaches where appropriate

**Management Systems**

[ ] Create credentialing calendar with key dates
[ ] Develop tracking system for application status
[ ] Assign specific team member responsibility for credentialing
[ ] Implement contract management system
[ ] Identify key payor contacts
[ ] Schedule regular reviews of contracts and credentials

**Outsourcing Assessment**

[ ] Evaluate whether to use Credentialing Verification Organization (CVO)
[ ] Compare costs ($400–$1000 per provider) against potential revenue loss from delays
[ ] Consider hybrid approach (outsource initial credentialing, handle maintenance in-house)
[ ] Determine if contract negotiation assistance is needed for major payors

**Ongoing Management**

[ ] Create master calendar for license renewals, board certification, DEA registration
[ ] Set up alert system for CAQH attestation updates
[ ] Schedule Medicare and Medicaid revalidation reminders
[ ] Plan for contract renegotiation 6–9 months before renewal dates

# Chapter 12

# Malpractice Insurance

## Introduction

In virtually all business situations, there is a need to have insurance. Much of this is related to the litigious society in which we live, and the mechanisms by which persons use *contingency* lawsuits (where lawyers are paid only if they win a settlement) in order to capture damages. Medicine is no different, and in this case, since the public sees large sums of money documented in the lay press against physicians and providers, there is logic in trying to get settlements with such huge potential. The difficulty, of course, is that those settlements, which make patients wealthy, are a small numerator, and the fact is the (much) larger denominator results in *de minimus* settlements (or nothing for the plaintiff), much of which is taken by the contingency counsel. Nonetheless, the perception is still that doctors can be worthwhile targets, and malpractice insurance is a necessary component of your business – no matter if you are in private practice OR corporate practice.

## Types of Malpractice Insurance

Most of the time, the offering of malpractice coverage is "claims-made", rather than "occurrence". There is a significant difference between the two, so let's go over these so you understand what is being covered.

### *Occurrence*

This is the most expensive type of insurance available. Occurrence insurance is not time delimited, as long as you were covered by the insurance when the patient encounter occurred, hence the term. As a result, even if your insurance carrier changes, or you retire, if the incident occurred when the insurance was in effect, you are covered. As an example, if you had occurrence insurance through


DOI: 10.4324/9781003685623-12

May 5, 2035, after which you no longer see patients, and a patient sues you for something that happened on May 1, 2035, even though your policy is no longer in effect, you are still covered. With this type of policy, with standard coverage limits of $1M/$3M, you would have up to $1M to cover an incident that occurred during the policy year, and a total of $3M to cover all claims that result from incidents during the year.

The advantage of this type of policy is you don't have to renew your policy to maintain the coverage needed for any year during which you were insured. Because separate limits would exist for each year you were insured, no past claims will erode into the limits of subsequent coverage.

## Claims-Made

This is the most common insurance used in medicine; it is the cheapest at the outset, which is probably the reason most providers use it initially. In this type of insurance, you are ONLY covered if the claim made against you from a patient IS WHEN YOU ARE PAYING PREMIUMS. Here, the original inception date, that is, the "retroactive date", is the permanent part of the policy, wherein all claims to be covered must be on or after that date and during the time the policy is in effect. In the aforementioned scenario, if the patient sues for something that happened on May 1, and it's May 6, and your claims-made insurance is no longer in effect, you have no insurance at that point. The only insurance you have is when the claim was made at the time when a premium is being paid. As noted, while claims-made insurance is cheaper than occurrence at the outset, it gradually goes up in cost until a given time (i.e., five to seven years) when the cost increases dramatically; that's because underwriters feel your risk of getting sued is now considerably higher. By the way, this happens in other businesses also; it's called the "maturation period" where the longer you are in business, the more of a chance you have of getting sued. And this is a US phenomenon only – you won't find this in other countries since contingency lawsuits aren't permitted. While there is a statute of limitations for malpractice lawsuits, it varies by state, and there are many exceptions (e.g., alleged negligence or omission, concealment, and minor or incapacitated individuals).

The advantage of this type of policy is that you can change the coverage limits yearly, and it's certainly cheaper at the outset, prior to maturity. A subsequent policy (see below) can also be added later such that you can be protected when risk is ostensibly higher, with less cash burden when starting out in practice. The choice of going with occurrence vs. claims-made really depends on doing the math on anticipated changes at maturity, as well as the subspeciality you are pursuing and the rate of lawsuits therein. Your broker can help lay out the costs of both scenarios with you on an individual basis.

## Tail and Nose

So how do we insure ourselves? Obviously, the first step is to obtain the claims-made or occurrence insurance, with the claims-made the most frequent type of insurance. As you are beginning practice, the premiums aren't going to be *too* high, at least for the first few years. However, once you reach the maturity stage, you have two choices:

1. Buy *occurrence* insurance going forward, either on top of or in place of the claims-made insurance. This maximizes the chance that you will be covered for the time before maturity and subsequently going forward.
2. Obtain *tail* insurance. Tail insurance extends the time in which there is coverage for any claims-made subsequent to the time after which the policy expires. What tail insurance does

is convert the claims-made insurance, and any events occurring during the time the claims-made insurance was in effect, into an occurrence insurance as a supplement to the original policy. This can be time delimited, for example, for an ensuing five years after the claims-made original policy expires, or unlimited (the better option), which costs more and is usually 1.5 to 2.5× the last year's premium. This is typically a one-time payment, and your coverage is done for that period (especially if you are retiring or no longer seeing patients).

You should always check to see what the most reasonable cost approach would be – to have the occurrence policy or the claims-made with tail. Most physicians we know have a tail policy, since the starting process was a claims-made policy. However, we have seen that the total cost of a claims-made policy, with a tail added on, is very similar to an occurrence policy overall. A key point is that some claims-made policies offer no additional cost tail coverage for death, disability, or permanent retirement – check and/or negotiate for these details.

Since some of you will be coming from an old practice to a new one, the concept of *nose* insurance comes up. Tail insurance often is available from the insurer that covered you for the claims-made policy; it's the supplement to cover what they covered before when you paid a premium. If you're coming from a previous job, they may cover tail insurance for you or at least offer tail insurance for the patients treated in your previous practice. That's wise to obtain, since you'll be leaving the previous practice and thus won't be part of the policy any longer.

But what if there is NO tail insurance? What can you do then? Well, you can purchase *nose* insurance. Nose insurance is "prior acts coverage", viz., covering the time you were with the other group. This is essentially your tail insurance if it were available from your previous insurer; but since they didn't offer it, you have to make sure you have coverage for the time you were in that previous practice. Similar to tail insurance, the cost is usually some multiple of a previous premium; there is a retroactive date, here called a *prior acts date*, where the new carrier insures you back to that date. It's kind of the reverse of a tail, by making sure you are covered for the time when you were working in previous practices.

## Documentation and Standard of Care

One key strategy to avoid malpractice issues is documentation. Our world is one of electronic documentation, and outlining what was discussed, the examinations and the conclusions made with clear documentation cannot be overemphasized. Luckily, today we have templates that can be used in our electronic medical records that ensure we have complete notes, but it is very clear that in some cases we rely upon them too heavily. Always be sure your notes are clear and articulate what you would want any audience OTHER THAN YOURSELF to know – after all, the notes aren't (just) for you, they're for *anyone else reading the chart, friend or foe*. That's the reality of the situation in the medical-legal framework in which we exist.

The note is your documentation of the patient encounter to the world – payors, patients, providers, and pariahs. Use it wisely.

The other aspect of our world is the *standard of care* doctrine. Regretfully, this is an oft cited and poorly understood aspect, since it is a *legal* concept, not a medical one. Standard of care is the ostensive benchmark for whether a professional standard has been met, and if not, the accusation of negligence. In our case, standard of care has been defined on a region-by-region basis, usually state by state. Many states follow the definition of a "national standard", as noted by Connecticut Code §52-184c: "… level of care, skill and treatment which, in light of all relevant surrounding circumstances, is recognized as acceptable and appropriate by reasonably prudent similar health care providers".

Something that should be clear is that this can be a relativistic aspect, but clearly attempting to be at the national standard is wise. What has been noted by various risk management groups is that standard of care is different from *optimal* care, since healthcare is a continuum, rather than an absolute. All patients are not the same, and care varies with regard to what is considered acceptable but at the lower or higher end of the spectrum. The courts have also noted the importance of clinical judgment (as long as the clear rationale has been documented!). There are a number of sources of determination of standard of care, from law, to regulations, to authoritative guidelines (although these also are relative), policies of national clinical institutions, journal articles, standards of accreditation, and local policies. For us, citing the clinical literature is something that we do quite frequently not only for academic interest, but also to ensure any audience understands the rationale of our work. Forewarned is forearmed; learning the details of how this applies to your specific situation from knowledgeable legal advisors is what we suggest.

## *A Happy Customer*

Unhappy patients, as noted in the chapter on CRM, will not be your most compliant patients. Needless to say, unhappy patients also sue. One of the key aspects of prevention of potential issues is CRM, and how you deal with patients from the moment they step into your office, see you on the computer screen, and/or interact with you in shared office space. Being attentive to the person-to-person interaction and leveraging this helps avoid misunderstandings and thus lawsuits.

We cannot prevent unfortunate results for some patients who are sick – part of the art of medicine is dealing with those who have medical hardships. But we can try to alleviate the suffering we see and not be wed to technology as a replacement for our compassionate interaction. One of us had an experience of a delay of diagnosis for all the wrong reasons – orders being lost, tests being delayed, follow-ups being cancelled, etc. In that case once the diagnosis, and subsequent treatment, was effected, I took ten minutes and apologized to the patient and her daughter, taking the lion's share of the culpability. The patient was silent for a moment and graciously acknowledged the apology noting her appreciation that her caregiver was taking responsibility. She was one of the best patients subsequently, and despite the potential for legal issues, was assuaged with the apology.

Acknowledging the hurdles the patient has had to jump through may be the most compassionate thing you do; it may also prevent a lawsuit.

# Chapter 13

# Selecting the Right EHR/EMR for Your Practice

## Introduction

Choosing the right electronic health record (EHR) or electronic medical record (EMR) system is an important decision that shapes everything from day-to-day operations to long-term financial health and patient outcomes.

The EHR becomes the central nervous system of a medical practice, touching virtually every process from scheduling and documentation to billing and clinical decision support. When implemented effectively, these systems can dramatically streamline workflows, reduce administrative burden, and help providers deliver more consistent, compassionate care.

Practices that select an EHR aligned with their specialty needs and style often see tangible benefits: reduced documentation time, fewer missed billing opportunities, decreased medication errors, and improved care coordination. The right system can also facilitate meaningful patient engagement through secure messaging and portal access to records.

However, a poor EHR choice can have equally significant negative impacts – creating frustration, increasing workload, and potentially compromising patient care. That's why it's essential to approach this decision strategically, considering factors like specialty-specific functionality, interoperability with other systems, user experience design, vendor support quality, and total cost beyond just the initial purchase price.

The investment in selecting the right EHR pays dividends over many years, while correcting a mistake often requires substantial resources and disruption to practice operations.

Healthcare technology continues to evolve rapidly, with new features, integration capabilities, and regulatory requirements emerging constantly. Understanding this technology will help you succeed in your new private practice. This guide provides a framework for evaluating EHR/EMR systems based on criteria that align with long-term practice success.


DOI: 10.4324/9781003685623-13

## Key Features to Look for

### *Usability and Workflow Integration*

The usability of your EHR system will directly impact your satisfaction, productivity, and, ultimately, quality of care. According to a study in Mayo Clinic Proceedings, physicians who reported poor EHR usability were 2.8 times more likely to experience symptoms of burnout. When evaluating potential systems, pay special attention to customizable templates that can be tailored to your unique practice patterns. Customizable templates can reduce documentation time by up to 25%.

Look for systems that are easy to use. The best systems require minimal clicks to complete common tasks, ideally 1–3 clicks for routine functions. You may want to access patient information across multiple settings, making mobile accessibility a crucial feature. Cloud-based EHRs with mobile interfaces allow for clinical documentation and decision-making at the point of care, improving both efficiency and accuracy.

Voice recognition capabilities have become increasingly important as they can significantly reduce typing. Voice-enabled documentation can save physicians an average of 5.5 minutes per patient encounter. When evaluating an EHR's usability, arrange for multiple staff members to participate in demonstrations using patient scenarios specific to your specialty. This hands-on experience will provide far more insight than vendor presentations alone.

An alternative approach involves the use of an AI agent, that can be integrated into your EHR system to provide services, including generating progress notes, assigning correct diagnostic codes, and managing prescriptions. This option will be discussed further later in this chapter.

### *Interoperability*

Healthcare delivery increasingly occurs across a distributed network of providers, requiring seamless information exchange. Systems with robust interoperability capabilities ensure your practice can communicate effectively with other systems.

Consider participation in national health information exchanges like *CommonWell Health Alliance* and *Carequality*, which significantly expands your ability to access patient records from other healthcare organizations. Systems certified for these networks can dramatically reduce information gaps during care transitions. Ask potential vendors about their participation in these networks and whether additional fees apply.

*Direct Secure Messaging*, an email-like standard that allows for encrypted communications containing protected health information between authorized providers, facilitates referrals, care coordination, and transitions of care. Ensure your chosen system includes this capability as a standard feature, not an expensive add-on.

Remember that true interoperability goes beyond technical capability to include business arrangements and policies. Even if a system can technically exchange information, vendor policies or additional costs might create barriers. Ask vendors about their policies on data sharing and any associated costs.

### *Patient Engagement Tools*

Today many patients expect digital access to their healthcare information and services. Many patient engagement tools not only meet these expectations but also improve health outcomes and practice efficiency.

Your EHR should include a patient portal that allows patients to view their health information, schedule appointments, request medication refills, and communicate securely with providers. Active portal users have been found to have 8–12% higher medication adherence rates. When evaluating portals, consider the patient experience – overly complex portals are generally used less often, despite their technical capabilities.

Since the COVID-19 pandemic, telehealth capabilities or integration with telehealth platforms have expanded. The best systems support virtual encounters. Ask vendors to demonstrate their telehealth workflow from both the provider and patient perspective to ensure it meets your practice needs.

Appointment reminders using text, email, and voice channels have been shown to reduce no-show rates by 30–40%. The most effective systems allow for customized reminder timing and frequency based on appointment type and patient preferences. Explore whether these reminders can be automated.

## Compliance and Security

Healthcare remains one of the most heavily regulated industries, with significant penalties for data breaches and compliance failures. Your EHR must provide up-to-date security features while assuring regulatory compliance.

The Health Insurance Portability and Accountability Act (HIPAA) establishes standards for protecting sensitive patient information. Your EHR should implement required safeguards, including access controls, audit trails, and encryption of data. During vendor evaluations, ask for specific documentation about their HIPAA compliance measures and any history of security incidents.

Your system should allow permission settings to ensure staff members can access only the information necessary for their specific jobs, reducing the risk of unauthorized access or data breaches. The best systems allow you to customize these settings to match your practice's organizational structure.

Multifactor authentication (MFA) adds an essential security layer by requiring multiple verification methods to establish user identity. This has become a standard security expectation and is increasingly required by cybersecurity insurance providers.

Your EHR system needs backup plans in case something goes wrong. This means your data should be saved in multiple locations far away from each other, so if there's a problem in one place (like a natural disaster), your practice can still function.

Make sure your vendor automatically backs up your data regularly and can tell you exactly how long it would take to get your system back up and running after a problem. Don't just take their word for it – ask them about real situations where they've had to recover data, and how long it actually took. Companies often promise quick recovery times in theory, but what happens in real emergencies is what truly matters for your practice.

Your EHR vendor needs to have a clear plan for handling data breaches. Ask them exactly what they'll do if someone unauthorized accesses your patients' information. They should show you their step-by-step plan for responding to security problems, including how they'll notify you and affected patients as required by law.

You may want to request to see their actual breach response plan in writing. Check if it matches what your practice needs, especially how quickly they'll tell you about problems and how they'll fix them.

Remember that even the best security technology can be undermined if your staff doesn't follow proper security practices. Make sure to include security training for everyone in your practice as part of your EHR implementation plan.

## Making Better Healthcare Decisions with Data

As healthcare continues to shift toward value-based care models, your system should be capable of analyzing patient populations by various risk factors, identifying where care might be lacking and enabling proactive interventions. The best systems integrate both clinical information and social determinants of health, recognizing that factors like housing stability and income significantly impact health outcomes and costs.

Quality reporting shouldn't create additional administrative burden. Look for systems that automatically calculate and submit measures for programs like MIPS (Merit-Based Incentive Payment System – a program within the US healthcare system that rewards healthcare providers for delivering high-quality, cost-effective care to Medicare beneficiaries) to help secure incentive payments. Effective systems don't just provide retrospective reports – they alert providers to quality gaps during patient visits when intervention is still possible.

Finally, when assessing reporting capabilities, bring examples of reports you currently rely on or wish you had. Ask vendors to demonstrate how these reports would be generated in their system, noting whether this requires specialized programming or can be accomplished using standard tools accessible to your staff. This practical approach will help ensure the system truly meets your practice's unique needs.

## Understanding the Financial Side of EHR Systems

When choosing a new EHR system, you need to look beyond the initial price tag. A complete financial analysis should consider all expenses you'll face over the next five years, including implementation costs, computer equipment, monthly or yearly fees, connection costs to other systems, staff training time, and temporary slowdowns during the transition period. It's important to ask vendors to provide a detailed breakdown of all these costs, including any planned fee increases after your initial contract period.

A well-implemented system can provide significant return on investment through various mechanisms. EHRs typically lead to better capturing of billable services (2–7% increase), fewer denied insurance claims (10–30% reduction), eliminated transcription costs, and more efficient staffing. When evaluating systems, request examples from practices similar to yours that demonstrate these financial benefits and provide a realistic timeline for achieving them.

EHR systems typically offer different payment structures that impact your long-term costs. While subscriptions with monthly per-provider fees seem cheaper at first, they often cost more than perpetual licenses (which have a larger upfront cost with yearly maintenance fees) over a five-to-seven-year period. Usage-based systems, where costs vary based on system utilization, represent a third option. It's worthwhile to calculate the breakeven point based on your practice's specific growth plans.

Contract flexibility is another crucial consideration. It is important to ensure that your contract allows for changes as your practice evolves. Carefully review termination clauses and data ownership provisions, paying special attention to any fees for extracting your data if you switch systems later.

Proper implementation support greatly affects how quickly you'll see benefits from your EHR investment. Comprehensive project management, data migration assistance, workflow analysis, and thorough training are critical success factors. When comparing vendors, understand exactly which support services are included in the base price vs. what costs extra. Speaking with client references provided by the EHR company about their implementation experience can help you learn about unexpected costs.

When calculating your return on investment, consider both direct financial benefits and indirect benefits like improved work–life balance for your team. These indirect benefits can reduce staff turnover and recruitment costs, which are significant in today's healthcare job market. Involving your financial advisor or healthcare consultant when evaluating vendors can ensure all cost factors are properly considered and lead to a more successful EHR implementation.

## AI Agents for Medical Offices

Medical practices today are increasingly turning to AI solutions to address administrative challenges and enhance patient care. Modern healthcare AI agents, such as and Olive Health, serve as virtual assistants that seamlessly integrate into clinical workflows, offering capabilities that extend far beyond basic automation.

These sophisticated AI systems function as virtual medical scribes during patient encounters, actively listening to and transcribing conversations between physicians and patients. Unlike traditional transcription services, AI agents process relevant clinical information and organize it into structured documentation that aligns with medical best practices. These systems can identify key symptoms, diagnoses, and treatment plans discussed during appointments then generate comprehensive notes that can be directly incorporated into EHRs.

AI systems can also automate routine administrative tasks and streamline workflows. These systems handle insurance verifications, process prior authorizations, and conduct eligibility checks without human intervention, while virtual assistants manage appointment scheduling and common patient inquiries. The AI's ability to analyze claims data reveals denial patterns and revenue cycle inefficiencies, providing insights for financial optimization. By eliminating these administrative burdens, healthcare providers can focus on delivering exceptional patient care rather than managing paperwork, creating more patient-centered medical practices.

The advantages of implementing AI assistants in a medical practice are substantial. They dramatically reduce the administrative burden on healthcare providers who typically spend hours each day on documentation. By automating this process, physicians can redirect their attention to patient care, potentially seeing more patients or simply having more meaningful interactions with each person they treat. This shift not only improves the patient experience but also helps combat physician burnout.

From a financial perspective, AI can suggest appropriate medical codes based on the content of each visit. This intelligent coding assistance helps maximize appropriate reimbursement while reducing the risk of coding errors that could lead to claim denials or compliance issues. These systems continuously learn from coding patterns and feedback, becoming increasingly accurate over time.

However, implementing an AI agent requires careful consideration of several factors. Privacy and security are paramount concerns, as these systems process sensitive patient information. Medical practices must ensure that any AI solution they adopt complies with HIPAA and other relevant regulations. Additionally, there's a question of how the technology integrates with existing systems – compatibility with the practice's EHR platform is essential for seamless operation.

Training requirements also need to be considered. While modern healthcare AI is designed to be intuitive, staff will need time to become comfortable with the technology and learn how to maximize its benefits. Practices should account for this learning curve when implementing any new AI system.

Cost is another important factor. While the long-term return on investment may be substantial through improved efficiency and billing accuracy, the initial implementation and ongoing subscription fees represent a significant commitment. Practices must weigh these costs against projected benefits when deciding whether to adopt such technology.

As medical practices continue to deal with increasing administrative demands while striving to maintain quality patient care, AI agents can potentially transform how healthcare is delivered and documented.

## EHR/EMR Selection Checklist

### Usability and Workflow Integration

[ ] Evaluate customizable templates
[ ] Count clicks required for common tasks (aim for 1–3 clicks for routine functions)
[ ] Test mobile accessibility for point-of-care documentation
[ ] Assess voice recognition capabilities
[ ] Arrange for multiple staff members to participate in hands-on demonstrations
[ ] Test the system with patient scenarios

### Interoperability

[ ] Verify participation in national health information exchanges
[ ] Confirm Direct Secure Messaging capabilities
[ ] Ask about any additional fees for information exchange features
[ ] Review vendor policies on data sharing between systems
[ ] Check compatibility with other healthcare organizations

### Patient Engagement Tools

[ ] Evaluate patient portal functionality (appointment scheduling, refill requests, secure messaging)
[ ] Test portal usability from the patient perspective
[ ] Assess telehealth capabilities
[ ] Review appointment reminder options (text, email, voice) and customization features
[ ] Check if automated reminders are included or require additional fees

### Compliance and Security

[ ] Request documentation of HIPAA compliance measures
[ ] Review permission settings and role-based access controls
[ ] Confirm multifactor authentication availability
[ ] Evaluate data backup procedures and disaster recovery timelines
[ ] Review the vendor's data breach response plan

**Data Analytics and Reporting**

[ ] Verify automatic quality measure calculation for programs like MIPS
[ ] Check if the system can identify care gaps during patient visits
[ ] Bring examples of reports you need and verify they can be created
[ ] Determine if custom reports require specialized programming or external consultants

**Financial Considerations**

[ ] Request detailed five-year cost breakdown (implementation, hardware, subscriptions, interfaces)
[ ] Compare different payment models (subscription vs. perpetual license vs. usage-based)
[ ] Calculate the breakeven point based on your practice's growth plans
[ ] Review contract flexibility, termination clauses, and data ownership provisions
[ ] Understand which implementation services are included vs. additional

**AI Integration Capabilities**

[ ] Evaluate AI documentation assistance features
[ ] Check compatibility with third-party AI solutions
[ ] Assess coding assistance capabilities for improved reimbursement
[ ] Review privacy and security measures for AI features
[ ] Understand training requirements for AI implementation

**Implementation and Support**

[ ] Speak with reference clients about their implementation experience
[ ] Review training options for providers and staff
[ ] Ask about ongoing technical support
[ ] Inquire about the vendor's update schedule and how updates are deployed
[ ] Develop a transition plan to minimize disruption to practice operations

# Chapter 14

# Mastering Medical Coding for Your Private Practice

## Introduction

Let's talk about something that might sound boring but could make or break your private practice: medical coding. It happens time and again – the difference between thriving practices and struggling ones often comes down to this seemingly mundane aspect of healthcare. As you make that exciting leap from residency or corporate practice to running your own show, understanding medical coding becomes not just some administrative headache but a cornerstone of your business model. We're here to demystify this complex world and give you the practical knowledge you need to optimize your revenue cycle from day one. While we have had the experience of learning these codes through our own practice, there are now courses offered to help gain familiarity with these systems – it's something to consider if you have limited familiarity to these alphabet soup acronyms. Because of the complexity and frequent changes, ensure that you understand the coding world and make sure your billing team is up to speed with all the changes, *and* educates you on those changes.

## The Foundation: Understanding Coding Systems

### *CPT Codes: Your Services Translated*

Think of Current Procedural Terminology (CPT) codes as the language through which you communicate your services to payers. The American Medical Association (AMA) developed and maintains these codes, and as a new practice owner, you'll want to become intimately familiar with the ones relevant to your specialty.

Most commonly used CPT codes fall into three categories. Category I includes the standard codes for procedures, services, and evaluations. Category II codes are optional and help track performance,

DOI: 10.4324/9781003685623-14

such as documenting a patient's most recent blood pressure. Category III codes represent emerging technologies and services.

Here's a practical tip: Create a "cheat sheet" of the most common CPT codes and diagnoses used in your specialty. Keep the list in a separate document file, with definition requirements, on your computer used for your notes. Trust us, this simple step will save you countless headaches down the road. Notably, today there are programs/apps (e.g., Ingenious Med) in which you can add a diagnosis and the CPT code will automatically come up. This has simplified and aided coding issues so that you don't have to memorize all the codes – use the diagnosis instead. But for the more common ones used in your practice, most likely you will get to know the codes.

### ICD-10-CM: Justifying Medical Necessity

Now let's talk about International Classification of Diseases, 10th Revision, Clinical Modification (ICD-10-CM) codes. These describe diagnoses and conditions and validate the medical necessity of your services to insurance companies.

Unlike CPT codes, ICD-10-CM codes get much more specific and detailed. Consider a simple forearm fracture – it might have dozens of potential codes depending on which bone, which part of the bone, whether it's displaced, and whether it's the initial or subsequent encounter. It's like the difference between saying "car" and specifying "red 2019 Honda Civic with leather seats and a sunroof".

Many practices fall into the trap of coding with unspecified codes (those ending in .9) when more specific codes are available. This can lead to claim denials, something you want to avoid since it costs you time and effort as well as your billing company's. *Always code to the highest level of specificity documented in your notes.* Most of the templates we've seen in the electronic medical record will help you with this.

### HCPCS Level II Codes: Beyond CPT

Healthcare Common Procedure Coding System (HCPCS) Level II codes cover services, supplies, and equipment not included in CPT. These become particularly important if you administer medications in the office, provide durable medical equipment, offer ambulance services, or use certain prosthetics or orthotics.

An important point: Many practices leave money on the table by not properly utilizing HCPCS codes for supplies and services that could be billed separately. Don't make this mistake – review these up front to ensure if your services are eligible, you code for it! For example, oncologists frequently give chemotherapy; some of the most common HCPCS codes are for administration of such drugs. So, for example, **J9355** *Injection, trastuzumab, excludes biosimilar, 10 mg* is the HCPCS II code for administration of trastuzumab branded drug, not the biosimilar. There would also be a fee for the purchase of the drug as well.

## Evaluation and Management (E/M) Coding: Where the Money Is

For most *non*-procedural specialties, E/M codes represent the bread and butter of your practice. In 2021, significant changes were made to E/M coding, shifting from a system that counted history and exam elements to one that emphasizes medical decision-making (MDM) or time.

## *Understanding the New E/M Guidelines*

Under current guidelines, the level of E/M service can be determined by either the level of MDM (straightforward, low, moderate, or high complexity) *or* total time spent on the date of encounter (including non-face-to-face time such as reviewing records).

When it comes to MDM elements, think about the number and complexity of problems addressed, the amount and/or complexity of data reviewed and analyzed, and the risk of complications, morbidity, or mortality. Again, in your own practice to date it's likely you've put things into categories in the assessment and plan, which will help structure the level of complexity in which the patient entails. By having a cheat sheet by the side of your computer you'll be able to see what level of E/M service is billable by either complexity or time. *Remember, any time you've spent reviewing the chart is part of the overall time to document!* This will often be something that will push your billing up because of the need to see the patient's previous history.

Here's a documentation strategy we recommend: Structure your notes to clearly demonstrate the complexity of decision-making. For example, explicitly document your analysis of competing diagnoses or interpretation of tests, ensure you explain what your plan is due to the analysis, and don't forget to take into account the time you reviewed the chart *before and after* you saw the patient. We often document the total time spent with language that notes it includes both the time with the patient and the time needed to review the chart. This makes the level of service you're billing for crystal clear.

## *Avoiding E/M Coding Errors*

There are several common errors that can trigger audits. Most of these are common sense, but avoiding the errors is relevant because they become a time sink in dealing with appeals for denials, and there can be punitive actions as well if this is a pattern within your practice. At the outset, speaking with either a billing consultant or the billing firm you hire can be helpful in defining how these errors are flagged. Moreover, seeing examples by searching online can be helpful, although they may be older and not explicitly related to your current situation or practice. The key is to understand the billing components and fulfill these in your documentation. The common errors include:

1. *Upcoding* is consistently billing higher levels than supported by documentation. It doesn't matter if this is inadvertent; be clear on the complexity definitions and the time required.
2. *Unbundling* means billing separately for services that should be included in a single code. This is often seen in procedures that are done on the same day as an office visit. Hence, the reason you need to know coding is to be sure you can bill for each of these things separately.
3. *Copy-pasting* – using identical documentation across multiple patients – is a big red flag to auditors. This is also true for the *same* patient; we have seen uninformed doctors believing they can continue to bill in the hospital by copy-pasting their previous note day-in-day-out and be surprised that they are denied for all but the original note.
4. *Inadequate documentation*, failing to support the level of service billed, is the most common issue of all. This is of course due to ignorance; know what you need to document in order to be paid!

To protect yourself, consider periodic self-audits or hiring an external auditor to review a sample of charts periodically to identify potential compliance issues. Think of it as preventive medicine for your practice's financial health.

## E/M Modifiers: Fine-Tuning Your Claims for Maximum Reimbursement

E/M modifiers, or modifiers for short, are two-character codes that provide additional information about the services you've rendered without altering the fundamental meaning of the procedure code. Think of them as adjectives that add essential context to your coding "sentences". Using modifiers correctly serves three critical functions: preventing claim denials, ensuring appropriate reimbursement, and maintaining compliance. Let's dive deeper into how mastering modifiers can transform your practice's revenue cycle.

## Essential Modifiers Every Practice Should Know

### *Modifier 25: Significant, Separately Identifiable E/M Service*

**Definition:** Modifier 25 indicates that on the same day as a procedure or service, the patient's condition required a significant, separately identifiable E/M service above and beyond the usual pre- and post-operative care associated with the procedure.

**When to use it:**

When a patient presents for an office visit AND receives a procedure during the same encounter
When the E/M service goes beyond the standard work-up for the procedure

**Example:** A patient schedules a visit for wart removal (17110). During the examination, you also evaluate their hypertension, adjust medications, and order relevant labs. You would code:

17110 (Destruction of benign lesions)
99213-25 (Office visit, moderate complexity with modifier 25)

**Documentation requirements:** Your note must clearly establish that:

The E/M service was significant and medically necessary
The E/M service was separate from the procedure
The documentation supports the level of E/M service billed

**Common mistake:** Using modifier 25 when the only service provided was related to the procedure. Remember, the E/M service must address a separate issue or demonstrate complexity beyond what's normally required for the procedure.

### *Modifier 59: Distinct Procedural Service*

**Definition:** Modifier 59 indicates that a procedure or service was distinct and independent from other services performed on the same day. It's used to identify procedures not normally reported together but appropriate under specific circumstances.

**When to use it:**

Different session or encounter on the same day
Different procedure or surgery

Different site or organ system
Separate incision/excision
Separate lesion
Separate injury

**Example:** A dermatologist removes two lesions from different anatomic sites. The first is a malignant lesion on the face (11641), and the second is a benign lesion on the back (11401). You would code:

11641 (Excision malignant lesion face, 0.6–1.0 cm)
11401-59 (Excision benign lesion trunk, 0.6–1.0 cm with modifier 59)

**Documentation requirements:** Your documentation must clearly identify:

Different anatomical sites or body systems
Separate sessions if performed on the same day
Different lesions or injuries
Medical necessity for each procedure

**Revenue impact:** Failing to use modifier 59 when appropriate can result in the second procedure being denied as "bundled" with the first procedure – a potential loss of thousands of dollars annually.

**Important note:** Medicare now offers more specific modifiers (XE, XS, XP, XU) to replace modifier 59 in many situations. Check with your Medicare Administrative Contractor (MAC) for specific guidance.

## *Modifier 24: Unrelated E/M Service During Postoperative Period*

**Definition:** Modifier 24 indicates that an E/M service was provided during a global surgical period but was unrelated to the procedure.

**When to use it:**

When you see a patient during a global period (typically 10 or 90 days after surgery)
When the visit addresses an issue completely unrelated to the surgery
When the visit isn't for normal postoperative care

**Example:** A surgeon performed an appendectomy (44950, 90-day global period) on a patient 45 days ago. The patient now presents with symptoms of bronchitis unrelated to the surgery. You would code:

99213-24 (Office visit, moderate complexity with modifier 24)

**Documentation requirements:** Your note must clearly:

State that the visit is unrelated to the surgical procedure
Document the specific condition being addressed
Demonstrate that the condition is distinct from any complication of the surgery

**Common mistake:** Using modifier 24 for visits related to complications of surgery, which are included in the global surgical package.

### *Modifier 22: Increased Procedural Service*

**Definition:** Modifier 22 indicates that a procedure was substantially more difficult or complex than typically expected.

**When to use it:**

When a procedure takes significantly longer than usual
When unusual events complicate the service
When additional skill, time, or risk factors are present

**Example:** A dermatologist removes a 2.5-cm lesion from a patient's nose (11642), but the procedure is complicated by the patient's severe Parkinson's disease tremors, requiring additional assistance and taking twice the usual time. You would code:

11642-22 (Excision malignant lesion face, 1.1–2.0 cm with modifier 22)

**Documentation requirements:** Documentation for modifier 22 must be exceptional. Include:

Detailed description of the complexity or difficulty
Additional time required (preferably as a percentage increase over normal)
Additional work performed
Supporting clinical findings that increased the complexity

**Revenue impact:** When properly documented, modifier 22 can increase reimbursement by 20–30% for eligible procedures.

**Important note:** Always submit detailed documentation with claims using modifier 22. Many payers require operative notes attached to the claim.

## Additional Critical Modifiers Worth Mastering

### *Modifier 26: Professional Component*

**Definition:** Modifier 26 indicates that you're billing only for the professional component (interpretation) of a procedure that has both technical and professional components.

**Example:** A family physician interprets an ECG performed in the hospital using hospital equipment. You would code:

93000-26 (ECG with interpretation and report, professional component only)

### *Modifier 51: Multiple Procedures*

**Definition:** Modifier 51 indicates multiple procedures performed during the same session.

**Example:** An orthopedic surgeon performs both a carpal tunnel release (64721) and trigger finger release (26055) during the same operative session. You would code:

64721 (Carpal tunnel release)
26055-51 (Trigger finger release with modifier 51)

### *Modifier 50: Bilateral Procedure*

**Definition:** Modifier 50 indicates a procedure performed on both sides of the body during the same operative session.

**Example:** An otolaryngologist performs myringotomy with tube insertion on both ears. You would code:

69433-50 (Tympanostomy with anesthesia with modifier 50)

### *Modifier 57: Decision for Surgery*

**Definition:** Modifier 57 is used when an E/M service results in the initial decision to perform surgery.

**Example:** A patient presents to the emergency department with acute appendicitis. After evaluation, the surgeon decides to perform an appendectomy. You would code:

99285-57 (Emergency department visit, high complexity with modifier 57)
44950 (Appendectomy)

## Strategic Modifier Usage: Case Studies in Revenue Impact

### *Case Study 1: Primary Care Practice*

A primary care practice with five providers implemented a focused modifier education program, particularly emphasizing proper use of modifier 25. After three months:

Claim denials decreased by 32%
Average reimbursement per visit increased by $12
Annual revenue increased by approximately $78,000

**Key intervention:** They created an electronic health record (EHR) template that prompted providers to document separately identifiable E/M services when certain procedure codes were entered.

### *Case Study 2: Dermatology Practice*

A three-provider dermatology practice audited their modifier usage and found they were underutilizing modifiers 59 and 51 for multiple lesion removals. After implementing corrective measures:

Reimbursement for multiple procedures increased by 40%
Annual revenue increased by $94,500
No increase in audit frequency was observed

**Key intervention:** They developed a photographic documentation system that clearly identified multiple lesion locations and characteristics.

## Common Modifier Errors and How to Avoid Them

### *Error 1: Incorrect Modifier Sequencing*

When using multiple modifiers, sequence matters. Payment modifiers (e.g., 26, 50, 59) should typically be listed before informational modifiers.

**Example:** For a bilateral diagnostic nasal endoscopy performed on the right and left sides, code:

31231-50-RT (incorrect sequencing)
31231-50 (correct coding – modifier 50 indicates bilateral; no need for RT/LT)

### *Error 2: Modifier Redundancy*

Using multiple modifiers that communicate the same information.

**Example:** Coding 27447-50-RT-LT (Total knee replacement with modifiers 50, RT, and LT) is redundant. The correct coding is simply 27447-50.

### *Error 3: Using Modifiers to Bypass NCCI Edits Inappropriately*

Attempting to use modifier 59 to bypass Medicare's National Correct Coding Initiative (NCCI) edits without proper clinical justification.

**Prevention strategy:** Create an NCCI edit checker in your practice management system that alerts billers when modifier 59 may be needed but requires documented justification.

## Implementing a Modifier Management Program

To maximize appropriate modifier usage in your practice:

**Create modifier cheat sheets** specific to your specialty
**Develop clear documentation templates** that support modifier usage
**Conduct quarterly modifier audits** to identify patterns of under or overuse
**Implement automated claim scrubbers** that flag potential modifier opportunities
**Track denial reasons related to modifiers** and provide targeted education

## Payer-Specific Modifier Guidelines

Remember that different payers may have varying requirements for modifiers. For example:

Medicare requires the use of specific X modifiers (XE, XS, XP, XU) in many cases where commercial payers still accept modifier 59

Some payers require specific documentation with modifier 22 claims
Certain MACs have local coverage determinations (LCDs) with unique modifier requirements

We recommend creating payer-specific modifier profiles in your billing system to automatically apply the correct modifier format based on the payer.

## Financial Impact: The Bottom Line on Modifiers

The financial impact of proper modifier usage cannot be overstated. Consider these statistics from a recent practice management study:

Practices using modifiers correctly see 15–20% fewer denials than those with poor modifier management
Proper use of modifiers 25 and 59 alone can increase practice revenue by 5–8%
A single missed modifier opportunity on an $150 procedure, occurring just twice weekly, results in over $15,000 in lost annual revenue

When you multiply this across multiple providers and procedures, the impact becomes substantial – often the difference between a struggling practice and a thriving one.

Remember: Modifiers are not merely coding details; they're powerful tools for communicating the unique circumstances of your patient encounters and ensuring your practice receives appropriate compensation for the valuable care you provide.

## Navigating Specialty-Specific Coding Challenges

### *Primary Care Coding Pearls*

In primary care, time management and comprehensive documentation are key. You'll want to leverage annual wellness visits and chronic care management codes. Properly code for preventive services with problem-oriented visits. And use transitional care management codes for posthospital care. Primary care physicians can increase their revenue by 15–20% just by mastering these specific coding opportunities.

### *Surgical Specialties: Global Periods and Beyond*

If you're in a surgical specialty, you'll need to contend with global period restrictions, typically 10 or 90 days after a procedure. You'll also deal with assistant surgeon billing, preoperative clearance documentation, and staged procedure coding. Understanding these nuances can make a substantial difference in your reimbursement.

### *Mental Health Coding Considerations*

For mental health practitioners, focus on assessment and testing codes, psychotherapy add-on codes with E/M services, appropriate time-based coding, and the distinctions between group and individual therapy. Mental health coding has its own unique complexities but mastering them leads to more predictable revenue.

## Building Your Coding Infrastructure

### *EHR Selection with Coding in Mind*

When selecting an EHR system, consider these coding-related features: built-in coding suggestions based on documentation, compliance checking tools, easily accessible coding references, customizable templates for your specialty, and integration with billing systems. Moreover, AI-based software now will not only compose your note for the EHR, it will also suggest a code for the visit. These are not panaceas but certainly are excellent suggestions to allow you to choose your system to maximize your productivity in helping with your coding.

Here's some implementation advice: During EHR implementation, customize templates that exist within your software to capture the specific elements needed for proper coding in your specialty. This upfront work pays dividends for years to come.

### *Hiring and Training Coding Personnel*

Deciding between in-house coders and outsourced services depends on your practice size and specialty. In-house coding gives you greater control and communication, familiarity with provider documentation patterns, and the ability to quickly address questions. Outsourced coding offers expertise across a wide range of situations, no need to manage staffing and training, and is often more cost-effective for smaller practices.

Either way, budget for ongoing coding education as regulations and codes change annually. This isn't a one-and-done training situation – it's an ongoing investment in your practice's financial health. By the way, if you think this will be taken care of if you went into a corporate practice, the reality is that it is NOT. If you don't learn coding for even corporate practices, you will be required to meet regularly with the coding and billing personnel at the practice to go over your coding – typically on your own time. You will be subject to training to code "more appropriately" so the coding staff do not have to continuously audit your charts. And if you're not producing enough revenue, you'll be evaluated for your coding activity to push revenues to "expected" levels.

## Compliance and Audit Preparation

### *Documentation Best Practices*

Your documentation must support the codes billed. You'll see in the malpractice chapter (Chapter 12) we specifically advocate detailed notes, that you are making for everyone else in the world *but* yourself. The documentation fulfills the requirements for your thought process articulated, your justification of your plan, and the justification of your price. Follow these principles:

If it's not documented, it didn't happen.
Avoid ambiguous abbreviations.
Document medical necessity clearly. Include your clinical reasoning.
Sign and date all notes promptly.
In all cases, discuss the assessment and plan with the patient, and ensure that you document their understanding.

Good documentation is like insurance – you may not need it often, but when you do, you'll be incredibly grateful you have it.

## Optimizing Reimbursement Through Better Coding

### *Reducing Claim Denials*

Claim denials from coding issues are the bane of the existence of a practice. As noted, they eat up time in review, they create huge amounts of work for reassessment, they require follow-up by the billing people (whether internal or external). And, you still have to follow up to make sure the denials are appealed appropriately, with opportunity cost as well as not being paid! Common coding-related denial reasons include missing or invalid modifiers, lack of medical necessity documentation, incorrect sequencing of diagnosis codes, and mismatched diagnosis and procedure codes. This is why your coding and billing people and you need to be on the same page in order to ensure you avoid some of these pitfalls. One good thing is that for your practice you will typically be using a handful of codes and will become quite facile with them and what you need to include for avoidance of denials. Of note – if you are consistently getting denials from a payor, who is seemingly doing this to delay payments on a regular basis, you need to ensure the payor is worth it or consider renegotiating the contract. Hence, claim denials can also be a red flag for you to ensure you're prioritizing those patients – and thus payers – who are the most valuable to you.

Create a tracking system for denials that identifies patterns and root causes, allowing you to address systematic issues. This proactive approach turns the frustration of denials into an opportunity for practice improvement.

### *Navigating Payer-Specific Requirements*

Different payers may have varying code edits and bundling rules, prior authorization requirements, modifier usage preferences, and documentation expectations. It's like each payer speaks a slightly different dialect of the same language. In general, most billing/coding services have an understanding of the subtleties of each payor; if they don't, they are *not* appropriate for your practice. We have seen software packages from these firms that pull out the key aspects of each patient encounter to ensure the appropriate documentation is present for a given payor. When evaluating a service, ensure they have the ability to be able to pull out such detail for your submission to avoid denials based on a key factoid.

Here's a payer strategy we recommend: Have the billing/coding service create payer-specific cheat sheets for you and your staff that outline the unique requirements of each major insurer you work with. This simple tool can dramatically reduce denials and payment delays.

## Staying Updated: Coding Changes and Resources

### *Annual Updates and How to Prepare*

Systems update annually, with changes effective January 1st. Prepare by reviewing code changes in your specialty (published in October–November), updating superbills (an itemized invoice or form that healthcare providers give to patients after receiving medical services) and EHR templates, training staff on new codes and guidelines, and adjusting fee schedules for new codes.

### *Essential Coding Resources*

You'll want to have access to several key resources: The AMA CPT® Professional Edition is the definitive source for CPT codes. The ICD-10-CM Official Guidelines are published by the Centers for Medicare and Medicaid Services (CMS). Many specialty organizations offer coding guides specific to their field. The Medicare Learning Network provides free resources on Medicare coding and billing. And you might consider coding software subscriptions like EncoderPro or TruCode. You'll want to ensure that annually before the next year starts you meet with your coding/billing people to set the stage with any "new" requirements.

## Conclusion: Coding as a Strategic Asset

Mastering medical coding is not merely about compliance or getting paid – it's about optimizing your practice's financial health. View coding as a strategic asset that allows you to capture the full value of the services you provide, reduce administrative waste from denied claims, minimize audit risk and compliance concerns, and create data-driven insights into your practice patterns.

By investing time in understanding coding principles and creating robust systems from the outset, you lay the groundwork for a financially sustainable and profitable private practice that can focus on what matters most: providing excellent patient care without losing money.

**Take these action steps:**

1. Identify and master the top CPT codes for your specialty.
2. Develop a compliance plan before seeing your first patient.
3. Establish relationships with coding experts in your specialty.
4. Schedule regular coding reviews during your first year.
5. Budget for ongoing coding education and resources.

Remember, in a profitable private practice, excellent clinical care and excellent coding go hand in hand – you cannot sustain one without the other. We both know practitioners who are brilliant clinicians but poor coders, and they struggle financially, while those who master both aspects build thriving practices. We want you to be in that second category.

## Medical Coding Checklist

**Foundation: Understanding Coding Systems**

[ ] Create a "cheat sheet" of most common CPT codes for your specialty
[ ] Learn key ICD-10-CM codes relevant to your practice
[ ] Identify HCPCS Level II codes that apply to supplies/services you provide

**Modifier Mastery**

[ ] Learn essential modifiers for your specialty (25, 59, 24, 22, etc.)
[ ] Create specialty-specific modifier reference guides
[ ] Develop documentation templates that support proper modifier usage

**Specialty-Specific Coding**

[ ] Research specialty society coding resources and guidelines
[ ] Understand global period implications (if applicable)
[ ] Master time-based coding requirements (if relevant to your specialty)

**Documentation Best Practices**

[ ] Structure notes to clearly demonstrate complexity of MDM
[ ] Document time spent (including non-face-to-face time) when relevant
[ ] Ensure documentation supports the level of service billed
[ ] Avoid copy-pasting and cloned documentation
[ ] Document medical necessity clearly for all services

**EHR and Coding Infrastructure**

[ ] Select an EHR with robust coding features
[ ] Customize EHR templates to capture elements needed for proper coding
[ ] Decide between in-house coding staff or outsourced services
[ ] Implement a claim denial tracking system

**Staying Updated**

[ ] Review annual code updates (published October–November)
[ ] Update superbills and EHR templates for new codes
[ ] Schedule annual meeting with billing/coding team to review changes

**Resources to Acquire**

[ ] AMA CPT® Professional Edition
[ ] ICD-10-CM Official Guidelines
[ ] Specialty-specific coding guides

# Chapter 15

# Mastering Medical Billing

## Introduction: Why Billing Matters More Than You Think

Let's have an honest conversation about medical billing. We know what you're thinking: "I spent over a decade in medical training to practice medicine, not to worry about billing codes". Trust us, we felt the same way when we started our practices. But here's the unvarnished truth – your clinical brilliance means absolutely nothing if your practice can't keep the lights on.

Many physicians who leave established positions to open their own practices discover this reality quickly. They provide excellent care to patients but barely cover their salaries because they don't understand billing. When these physicians master their billing processes, collections often double or triple – with the exact same patient volume.

The difference between a thriving private practice and one that fails often has less to do with clinical skills and more to do with understanding the business side – with medical billing sitting at the very center. This chapter will transform what seems like an administrative burden into a strategic advantage for your new practice.

## The Real Cost of Billing Ignorance

Before diving into the mechanics, let's understand what's at stake. The financial reality of medical billing errors is startling: the average practice leaves 5–10% of legitimate revenue uncollected due to billing errors, while up to 80% of medical bills contain errors of some kind. More concerning still, the typical small practice writes off between \$40,000 and \$100,000 in potential revenue annually due to avoidable billing mistakes. Something as simple as an incorrect modifier or missing documentation element can reduce reimbursement by 20–50%. For a new practice generating \$500,000 in annual revenue, this translates to \$25,000–\$50,000 left on the table – money that could fund a new staff position, upgrade your EHR, or simply increase your take-home pay.


DOI: 10.4324/9781003685623-15

Our medical schools and residency programs taught us how to manage complex medical conditions but didn't mention that using the wrong place of service code could cut reimbursement in half, potentially costing tens of thousands in lost revenue annually. These costly mistakes occur not from clinical incompetence but from gaps in billing knowledge.

Simply put, you can't afford not to understand billing.

## Your Billing Options: In-house, Outsourced, or Hybrid

One of your first decisions will be how to structure your billing operations. Each approach has merits and drawbacks.

With in-house billing, you'll have complete control over the billing process, enabling direct communication between clinical and billing staff without percentage-based fees to outside companies and allowing you to address issues immediately. However, this approach requires hiring, training, and managing dedicated billing staff. It also necessitates investment in billing software and clearinghouse connections, while creating additional compliance responsibilities for your practice and requiring significant personal oversight and understanding of billing processes.

If you choose outsourced billing, you'll benefit from expertise from specialists focused solely on revenue cycle management, reducing your need for billing staff and training. This approach often provides better performance metrics and analytics while decreasing the administrative burden on physicians. The downsides include typical costs of 5–8% of collected revenue, less control over the billing process, potential communication delays with clinical staff, and varying levels of service quality between billing companies.

Many successful new practices employ a hybrid model where front-end processes such as charge capture and coding review happen in-house, while back-end processes such as claim submission, payment posting, and denial management are outsourced. This allows the practice to maintain oversight while leveraging outside expertise.

Whichever model you choose, remember this fundamental truth: You don't need to process every claim yourself, but you absolutely must understand the process.

## The Billing Cycle: Following the Money

Medical billing isn't a single action but a cycle with multiple stages. Understanding this cycle is crucial whether you manage billing in-house or outsource it.

The billing cycle begins before the patient even arrives with patient registration and insurance verification. Proper registration includes demographic information collection, insurance verification (eligibility, coverage, deductibles), determination of patient financial responsibility, and prior authorization when required.

Here's a pro tip: Verify insurance 2–3 days before appointments for established patients and at scheduling time for new patients. This single step can reduce denials by up to 30%.

Next comes charge capture, the process of translating clinical services into billable events. This happens through encounter forms/superbills, EHR coding assistance, and charge entry from clinical documentation. Many new practices miss charges for services they consider "routine" or "quick", like wound checks or medication adjustments. These can represent significant revenue when properly captured.

As discussed in Chapter 14, coding translates your services into the language insurance companies understand, using CPT codes for procedures and services, ICD-10 codes for diagnoses, HCPCS codes for supplies and equipment, and modifiers that adjust code meanings. Remember, coding isn't just about compliance – it's about telling the complete story of your patient encounter. Under-coding is just as problematic as over-coding, and it costs many physicians thousands in legitimate reimbursement.

Once charges are coded, claims are submitted to payors through practice management software, clearinghouses that validate claims, and direct connections to payor portals. Your "clean claim rate" (percentage of claims accepted on first submission) should exceed 95%. Lower rates indicate systemic issues in your billing process.

When payments arrive, they must be posted to the correct patient accounts, reconciled against expected reimbursements, and analyzed for underpayments or denials. Payment posting might seem like simple bookkeeping, but it's actually a critical point for identifying payor patterns and problems.

After insurance pays their portion, patient statements are generated, payment options are offered, payment plans are managed when needed, and collections processes are initiated for nonpayment. Your billing materials and processes shape patient perception of your practice as much as clinical interactions do. *Clear, compassionate billing builds loyalty.*

When claims are denied, root causes must be identified, corrections must be made, appeals must be filed within tight deadlines, and systemic issues must be addressed. The average practice successfully overturns 60–70% of appealed denials, yet many physicians appeal less than 50% of denied claims – essentially giving away money they've earned. Again, forewarned is forearmed.

## Essential Billing Metrics: What You Must Monitor

Whether you handle billing in-house or outsource it, several key performance indicators should be on your *monthly dashboard* to ensure financial health.

*Days in Accounts Receivable* (DAR) measures how long it takes to get paid after providing service, with industry benchmarks at 30–40 days and a red flag threshold above 50 days. The real-world impact is significant: every day over the benchmark represents money not working for your practice. Reducing DAR from 50 to 35 days in a practice means collecting $40,000 monthly, which immediately adds $20,000 to your cash flow.

Your *Clean Claim Rate* – the percentage of claims accepted on first submission – should exceed 95%, with anything below 90% raising serious concerns. Each rejected claim costs approximately $25 in administrative time to correct and resubmit, not counting delayed payment.

The *Collection Ratio* represents the percentage of what you bill that you actually collect, with top practices maintaining 95–98% of contracted amounts. Dropping below 90% indicates potential problems with your fee schedule alignment or collection processes. This metric reveals whether your fee schedule aligns with contracted rates and if you're collecting what payors have agreed to pay.

*First-Pass Resolution Rate* measures the percentage of claims paid correctly on the first submission, with an industry benchmark above 85%. Claims requiring multiple submissions typically take 2–3 times longer to get paid, significantly impacting your cash flow.

Your *Denial Rate* (the percentage of claims denied by insurance) should stay below 5%, with rates exceeding 10% demanding immediate attention. When denial rates increase, categorize them by reason code to identify and address pattern issues in your billing process. Payors who consistently deny your otherwise clean billing should strongly be considered for renegotiation and/or termination.

## Billing Technology: Tools of the Trade

The right technology infrastructure can make or break your billing operations. Again, there are both in-house and outsourced solutions for these aspects.

*Practice Management Systems* (PMS) manage appointments, billing, and patient information. Key features should include electronic claims submission, insurance eligibility verification, patient statement generation, reporting and analytics, and integration with your EHR. When selecting a system, choose one with specialty-specific features. Psychiatrists need different billing functionality than surgeons.

Many modern EHR systems include billing features such as charge capture from clinical documentation, coding assistance and validation, claim scrubbing before submission, and integration with clearinghouses. The seamless flow of information between clinical documentation and billing significantly reduces errors and omissions. We definitely recommend considering such systems, as they are becoming standard in our world of practice.

*Clearinghouses* validate claims before submission to payors by checking for errors and missing information, verifying patient eligibility, submitting claims electronically, and providing tracking and reporting. While clearinghouse services typically cost $0.25–$0.50 per claim, they often pay for themselves by improving clean claim rates. As well, we have found that we can negotiate rates on the basis of the number of claims made to decrease the overall cost. Always be ready to negotiate!

*Patient payment platforms* facilitate patient payments through online payment portals, payment plan management, credit card processing, and mobile payment options. Practices offering multiple payment options typically collect 30% more at the time of service and report higher patient satisfaction – always consider the latest technology for payment – you never want to deny a patient's willingness to pay their bill!.

## Avoiding Common Billing Pitfalls

New private practices frequently encounter several predictable billing challenges that can significantly impact your bottom line.

*Inadequate documentation* remains one of the most frequent causes of claim denials, as clinical documentation must support every billed service. Implement documentation templates aligned with billing requirements for common procedures and visits, and review documentation against coding guidelines quarterly to prevent this issue.

*Under-coding out of fear* is surprisingly common among new practice owners who worry about audit risk. The balanced approach is to code accurately for the services actually provided, with documentation to support them. Don't leave money on the table due to unwarranted concern about audits when your documentation justifies the codes.

*Missing timely filing deadlines* can result in complete payment denial with no recourse. Each payor sets specific deadlines for claim submission, often ranging from 90 days to 1 year. Create a master calendar of these deadlines and implement a weekly review of unbilled services to avoid missing these critical windows.

Failure to *check eligibility* leads to significant wasted time and denied claims, as patient insurance changes frequently. Verify eligibility electronically before *every* visit, even for established patients, to prevent this common problem.

Ineffective patient collections stem from many physicians' discomfort discussing money with patients. Remember that clear financial conversations are actually part of good patient care. Script these conversations for your front desk team and practice them to ensure consistent, compassionate financial communication.

## Specialty-Specific Billing Insights

Different specialties have unique billing considerations that can dramatically affect your reimbursement and practice viability.

Primary care physicians need to focus on several key billing areas that can significantly enhance revenue. Chronic care management codes, annual wellness visits, preventive service coding, vaccination administration, and time-based billing for complex patients all represent important revenue streams. Properly billing for chronic care coordination (99490) alone can add $40–$50 per eligible patient monthly with minimal additional work, creating a substantial income source for practices with large numbers of chronically ill patients.

Surgical practices face distinct billing challenges centered around global period management, modifier usage for multiple procedures, assistant surgery billing, pre- and post-operative care modifiers, and implant and supply billing. A critical billing alert for surgeons: failing to append appropriate modifiers to secondary procedures can reduce reimbursement by 50–75%, potentially leaving thousands of dollars uncollected for each surgical case.

Mental health providers must pay careful attention to time-based service documentation, testing and assessment codes, appropriate use of evaluation vs. therapy codes, telehealth service billing, and insurance coverage limitations. For time-based therapy services, document both start/end times and total minutes to support the codes billed, as payers increasingly scrutinize these claims.

Other specialists, such as cardiologists and gastroenterologists, need to pay particular attention to diagnostic vs. therapeutic procedure distinctions, appropriate use of consultation codes, device and implant billing, facility vs. non-facility place of service coding, and technical vs. professional component billing. Understanding these distinctions is crucial – for example, the difference between diagnostic and therapeutic intent can significantly impact reimbursement for procedures like endoscopy, sometimes doubling the allowable amount.

## The Art of Patient Collections

One of the most challenging aspects of private practice is collecting from patients directly.

Your financial policy should be written in plain language, reviewed with patients before their first visit, signed and acknowledged, and consistently enforced. Frame your financial policy as ensuring the practice's ability to continue providing care, not as a punitive measure.

*The best time to collect is when service is provided.* Verify insurance and calculate patient responsibility *before* appointments, communicate expected payments when confirming appointments, train front desk staff in collection conversations, and offer multiple payment options (cash, check, credit cards, mobile payments). Practices that inform patients of expected costs 48 hours before appointments see 30% higher collection rates at the time of service. Remember, if you have to send a bill, something went wrong in the value chain of collections (and it's costing you and your practice)!

With deductibles rising, many patients face significant out-of-pocket costs. Use real-time eligibility verification to check deductible status, offer good-faith estimates before expensive procedures, consider payment plans for larger balances, and implement card-on-file programs. Train staff to discuss options compassionately: "I see you have a $3,000 deductible that hasn't been met yet. We estimate your portion of today's visit will be $275. How would you like to handle that today?"

Develop clear policies for financial hardship, including sliding fee scales based on income, payment plan options with reasonable minimums, hardship application processes, and charity care guidelines. Create systems that maintain practice viability while accommodating genuine financial need. There are a number of online suggestions to handle relative discounts as needed.

## Creating a Culture of Billing Excellence

The most successful private practices build billing awareness into their culture.

As the practice owner, your engagement with billing sets the tone. Review key billing metrics monthly, understand common denial reasons, participate in coding and documentation training, and recognize staff for billing successes. When physicians show interest in billing outcomes, staff prioritize billing accuracy and completeness. As noted in earlier chapters, allowing for "skin in the game" is a way to help everyone realize the importance of all staff in revenues and cost containment.

Invest in your team's billing knowledge through regular coding and documentation updates, specialized training for front desk on collections, clear processes for charge capture, and performance feedback based on measurable metrics. Consider performance bonuses tied to billing metrics like clean claim rate or time-of-service collections.

Foster regular communication between clinical and billing teams through weekly huddles addressing billing issues, shared access to denial and rejection data, collaborative problem-solving for recurring issues, and celebration of billing successes alongside clinical ones. Move from seeing billing as "administrative overhead" to recognizing it as the mechanism that funds your clinical practice.

## Learning the Language: Essential Billing Terms

To navigate billing effectively, you'll need to become fluent in several key terms that impact your reimbursement and practice management decisions.

The *allowed amount* represents the maximum a payor will reimburse for a service, regardless of what you charge. Strategically, you should know your top payors' allowed amounts for your most common services to set patient expectations accurately and make informed decisions about your fee schedule.

The *explanation of benefits (EOBs)* serve as the documentation from insurance companies detailing how claims were processed. These documents contain vital information needed to identify underpayments and improper denials, making them essential analytical tools rather than mere payment notices. Many billing and coding experts note that for a practice owner, this is THE most important thing to understand and review regularly to ensure you are receiving the appropriate reimbursement for services.

Understanding the difference between clearinghouse rejections and payor denials is crucial. A rejection occurs when a claim doesn't meet basic requirements for processing, while a denial means the claim was processed but payment was refused. This distinction matters because rejections require correction and resubmission, while denials require analysis and potential appeal – entirely different workflows with different timelines.

*E/M modifiers* – those two-digit codes that modify the meaning of procedure codes that we discussed in Chapter 14 – can dramatically affect your revenue. Appropriate modifier usage often makes the difference between denied and paid claims, particularly for surgical specialties where modifiers like -50 (bilateral), -51 (multiple procedures), or -59 (distinct procedural service) can significantly impact reimbursement.

Relative value units (RVUs) are units assigned to services reflecting work, practice expense, and liability. As many compensation models use RVUs to measure productivity, understanding them becomes essential for practice owners who need to evaluate provider performance and set compensation structures.

## Navigating Missed Appointment Billing

Missed appointments represent a significant financial burden for new practices, with the average no-show costing between $150 and $300 in lost revenue. Many physicians hesitate to implement missed appointment fees, fearing patient pushback. However, a well-structured missed appointment policy actually improves practice efficiency and patient accountability. Your missed appointment policy should clearly state the notice period required (typically 24–48 hours), the fee amount (usually 50–75% of the visit cost), and allowances for emergencies or first-time occurrences. Remember that most insurance plans won't cover missed appointment fees, so these charges will be the patient's responsibility. Document your attempts to contact the patient before the appointment, have patients acknowledge the policy in writing during onboarding, and apply the policy consistently to avoid accusations of favoritism. A pro tip from successful practices: implement a tiered approach where the first missed appointment receives a courtesy call and reminder of the policy, the second incurs a partial fee, and subsequent no-shows are billed at the full missed appointment rate. This balanced approach maintains the financial health of your practice while preserving positive patient relationships.

For appointment reminders, consider implementing a multi-touch system using automated text messages, emails, and phone calls that has been shown to reduce no-show rates by up to 30%. This is part and parcel of an excellent CRM system (see Chapter 9). Track your no-show data carefully to identify patterns – some practices discover that certain appointment slots have significantly higher no-show rates, allowing for strategic overbooking during these times. When billing for missed appointments, use clear language on statements such as "Missed Appointment Fee – [Date]" rather than clinical terminology. Finally, ensure your front desk team is comfortable explaining the policy with language like, "We reserve this time specifically for you and cannot fill it on short notice. Our missed appointment fee helps us maintain availability for all patients who need care". With these approaches, you can significantly reduce the financial impact of no-shows while maintaining positive patient relationships.

## The Personal Journey to Billing Mastery

Many physicians feel overwhelmed when first confronting billing complexities. Here's a roadmap to mastery.

Three months before opening your practice, focus on foundational understanding. Learn basic billing terminology, understand the revenue cycle, review your specialty's most common codes, and identify key metrics to track.

One to two months before you start seeing patients, develop your processes. Create documentation templates supporting proper coding, establish billing workflows, set up denial management processes, implement time-of-service collection strategies, and develop patient collection policies.

In the first month after your office is open, you are ready for optimization. Analyze patterns in denials and rejections, refine coding based on payor feedback, and begin regular billing performance reviews.

Your ongoing development should include quarterly coding updates, annual fee schedule reviews, regular audits of documentation and coding, and continuous refinement of patient collection approaches.

## Conclusion: Billing as a Clinical Skill

We want to leave you with this perspective shift: In private practice, billing isn't an administrative function separate from medicine – it's an extension of your clinical work. When you document thoroughly, code accurately, and ensure proper billing, you're completing the care cycle that began with the patient's first call to your office.

Learning billing is no different from learning a new surgical technique or treatment protocol. It requires practice. The physicians who embrace this reality find not only financial success but also greater autonomy in their practice.

Your excellence as a clinician deserves to be properly recognized and reimbursed. Mastering medical billing ensures that it will be.

For your next steps, identify your top most common procedures and learn their correct codes. Create a billing metrics dashboard to review monthly. Schedule time to understand your PMS's billing functions. Develop scripts for patient financial conversations. Consider which billing model (in-house, outsourced, or hybrid) best fits your practice.

Remember, you don't need to become a certified coder – you just need to understand billing well enough to lead your practice effectively. Your future financial stability depends on it.

## Medical Billing Checklist

### Foundational Understanding (Three Months Before Opening)

[ ] Review your specialty's most common procedure and diagnosis codes
[ ] Identify key billing metrics you'll need to track (Days in AR, Clean Claim Rate, etc.)
[ ] Research typical reimbursement rates for your top services in your geographic area

### Billing Structure Decision

[ ] Evaluate options: in-house, outsourced, or hybrid billing model
[ ] If outsourcing, interview multiple billing companies with experience in your specialty
[ ] If handling in-house, plan for staffing, training, and software needs
[ ] For hybrid approach, clearly define which functions stay in-house vs. outsourced

**Technology Infrastructure**

[ ] Select Practice Management System with specialty-specific features
[ ] Ensure EHR/PM integration for seamless charge capture
[ ] Set up clearinghouse relationships for electronic claims submission
[ ] Implement patient payment platforms with multiple payment options
[ ] Configure real-time eligibility verification capabilities

**Process Development (1–2 Months Before Opening)**

[ ] Create documentation templates that support proper coding for common services
[ ] Establish insurance verification workflow (2–3 days before appointments)
[ ] Create denial management and appeal processes with tracking system
[ ] Implement time-of-service collection strategies
[ ] Develop clear patient financial policies and payment options

**Patient Collection Systems**

[ ] Draft clear financial policy in plain language
[ ] Create process for reviewing financial responsibility with new patients
[ ] Develop scripts for front desk staff regarding collections
[ ] Set up multiple payment options (credit card, online, mobile)
[ ] Establish payment plan guidelines for larger balances
[ ] Develop financial hardship policies and application process

**Missed Appointment Management**

[ ] Create missed appointment policy with clear fee structure
[ ] Implement appointment reminder system
[ ] Train staff on consistent policy enforcement

**Staff Training**

[ ] Train front desk on insurance verification and patient collections
[ ] Create billing "cheat sheets" for common procedures and modifiers
[ ] Consider performance bonuses tied to billing metrics

**First Month Optimization**

[ ] Begin tracking key performance indicators (DAR, Clean Claim Rate, Collection Ratio)
[ ] Create system to analyze patterns in denials and rejections
[ ] Set up weekly billing meetings with clinical and billing teams
[ ] Establish monthly billing performance review

**Ongoing Monitoring**

[ ] Plan annual fee schedule evaluation
[ ] Set up regular audits of your billing processes
[ ] Regularly review EOBs to identify underpayments or pattern issues

**Specialty-Specific Considerations**

[ ] If primary care, set up systems for chronic care management codes and annual wellness visits
[ ] If surgical, establish processes for global period management and modifier usage
[ ] If mental health, create time-based service documentation templates
[ ] For all specialties, identify unique billing requirements and common pitfalls

# Chapter 16

# A Final Note

The journey to becoming a physician encompasses some of the most demanding learning that any of us have ever experienced. However, regardless of our given specialties, we've all made it through, and we've been taught, at the very least, to learn how to learn. One of the most satisfying things is to see how medicine has changed and how diseases that were once thought to be unapproachable we now can address ("treat") and/or have prolonged remissions ("cures"), and our growing armamentarium is something we continuously add to with our learning.

The practice of medicine today has changed with respect to the numbers of physicians in corporate practice. There are many reasons why there has been a shift over the past 30 or so years away from private toward corporate practice – it seemed more convenient, more lucrative, better for work–life balance. In some ways, this might have been true at the beginning. However, today the situation is much different.

Our experience has been seeing our colleague physicians experience some of the most profound levels and frequency of burnout due to the pressures of such corporate practice; the fear and antipathy and agitated depression with the constant piling of multitudes of tasks that are not related to good patient care, but instead processes designed for cost savings, at the cost of the provider. Virtually all physicians know of another who has taken their own life – a tragic consequence of a trajectory where corporate medicine cannot scale and literally costs workers their lives.

When discussing this with medical students, residents, fellows, and other physicians in large corporate/group practices, the theme has been the same – the lack of knowledge on how to start a practice given the lack of business training. One group we spoke to literally noted that if they knew the process to start a practice, they would all (four providers) give six months' notice. This lack of education is certainly a misstep in our current curriculum, but from which neither of us sees any resolution in the near future, despite attempts to the contrary.

Hence, the genesis of this book. With our involvement in the training of the next generation of physicians in medical school and in residency, and the lack of current guidance for students and


DOI: 10.4324/9781003685623-16

junior physicians, we felt it incumbent to provide a field guide to provide a choice, rather than the omnipresent thought that only joining corporate practice was possible. We don't disparage those who wish to work for large medical systems; far from it. For some, it is the right fit; after all, in the USA alone there will be a deficit of 50,000–100,000 physicians in the next five years. However, our goal is to remove a barrier to entry by which many physicians have expressed concern, not even knowing where to start, notwithstanding understanding the vocabulary of business. The irony is for anyone who has had to learn the brachial plexus, or who has had to use a Pfannenstiel-Kerr incision, or manage refractory hypertension, these concepts are frankly so much easier to learn, easier to implement, and less intense in execution in comparison. The majority of these processes, once set up, don't require constant attention as would a patient with COPD. And there are experts out there who can help in the processes that we can oversee. It is not so much a foreign land, where the natives aren't friendly, but rather one where the dialect is different, but there are interpreters who can help translate.

If you've read to this stage, you've done a lot of work already – creating a business plan with a marketing, finance, fundraising, operational set of plans – congratulations! You are ready to get to the next step, of executing your plans, of starting the practice. We hope that all that has been written here has helped with your journey, and if there were things that were missing, you'll let us know so we can fix that in future editions. We are, of course, ecstatic for you to continue your path, and we hope your successes provide you lasting professional joy and healthy outcomes to your patients. We also hope you'll drop us a line to let us know how you're doing.

We wish you the best of luck in *your* medical practice.

# Index

*Note*: Page numbers in **bold** indicate tables, and those in *italics* indicate figures.

## D